lonely planet

POCKET
NAPLES
& THE AMALFI COAST

Virginia DiGaetano

Contents

Above: Reggia di Caserta (p102);
Below: Naples (p33) with Mt Vesuvius in the distance

Plan Your Trip 4

The Journey Begins Here 4
Our Picks 6
Three Perfect Days 18
Get Prepared 22
When to Go 24
Getting There 26
Getting Around 27
A Few Surprises 30

POCKET NAPLES & THE AMALFI COAST

Explore Naples & the Amalfi Coast — 33

- Centro Storico — 35
- Toledo & Quartieri Spagnoli — 51
- La Sanità & Capodimonte — 65
- Santa Lucia & Chiaia — 77
- Capri Town & the Isle of Capri — 105
- The Amalfi Coast & Sorrento Peninsula — 119

Naples & the Amalfi Coast Toolkit — 141

- Family Travel — 142
- Accommodation — 143
- Food, Drink & Nightlife — 144
- LGBTIQ+ Travellers — 146
- Health & Safe Travel — 147
- Responsible Travel — 148
- Accessible Travel — 150
- Nuts & Bolts — 151
- Language — 152

FROM TOP: LEONID ANDRONOV/SHUTTERSTOCK ©, OLGA GAVRILOVA/SHUTTERSTOCK ©

★ Top Experiences

- Duomo di Napoli — 38
- Cappella Sansevero — 40
- Piazza Maradona — 54
- Palazzo Reale — 55
- Palazzo Reale di Capodimonte — 67
- Certosa e Museo di San Martino — 74
- Pompeii — 90
- Mount Vesuvius — 96
- Herculaneum (Ercolano) — 98
- Reggia di Caserta — 102
- Capri's Historic Villas — 108
- The Path of the Gods — 122
- Ravello — 124

PLAN YOUR TRIP

The Journey Begins Here

Congratulations! You've just made the very wise decision to visit the well-known but little-understood city of Naples, and untold treasures await. Its famously frantic energy is but the first layer in an almost mystical city full of ancient rituals and bursting with Mediterranean flavour. As if that weren't enough, the Amalfi Coast beckons, where jagged cliffs meet sapphire seas and a surprising amount of culture is ripe for discovery. Follow the Sirens' song along one of the world's most beautiful coastlines and hold on to your hats. It's a wild ride!

Virginia DiGaetano
@Cancel Anytime
Virginia figured out that the answers to the universe live in Naples, and she's not stopped going back since. Follow her Substack for this and other misadventures at @Cancel Anytime.

Sorrento (p132)
WITR/SHUTTERSTOCK ©

THE BEST

Museum Experiences

Naples has history on every corner, and you could spend days just wandering the city. But there are also museums bursting with treasures that should be on everyone's list.

Spend the day travelling from Ancient Egypt to the Bourbon dynasty at the **MANN**. (p58)

Explore the regal halls and Caravaggio canvases at the **Museo di Capodimonte**. (pictured above left; p67)

Learn about local traditions and history at the **Museo della Ceramica** in Vietri sul Mare. (p135)

Peruse contemporary art installations from international names at **MADRE**. (p45)

Line up at the **Cappella Sansevero** in the *centro storico* (historic centre) to see the iconic *Cristo Velato*. (p40)

Climb to the **Certosa e Museo di San Martino** for a panoramic view of Naples and centuries of local history. (pictured above right; p74)

Right: Museo Archeologico Nazionale di Napoli (MANN; p58)

THE BEST
Food and Wine Experiences

From vines and trees to fish and cheese, there is an enormous range of things to eat, drink and try around Naples and the coast that go way beyond pizza and pasta.

Join the Aceto farmers for their **Amalfi Lemon Experience** to learn how a family keeps growing for generations. (p133)

Get your cheese fix in Vico Equense where **Caseificio Starace** offers cheesemaking classes and tastings of the good stuff. (p133)

Dive into the fabled **Mercato della Pignasecca** in the Quartieri Spagnoli to haggle with grandmas over the freshest catch to land in Naples. (p57)

Hike Mount Vesuvius and see vineyards full of Lacryma Christi grapes, then taste varietals at **Sorrentino Vini**. (p97)

Head to **Cetara** to make *colatura*, the fish sauce that's been flavouring dishes since ancient Roman times. (p135)

Find your way to Furore where **Cantine Marisa Cuomo** offers incredible tastings on the Amalfi Coast. (p136)

From left: Lemons, the Amalfi Coast (p119); vineyard and Mt Vesuvius (p96); Seafood, Mercato della Pignasecca (p57)

Via San Gregorio Armeno (p30)

THE BEST

Shopping Experiences

We're well past cookie cutter souvenirs here – this is the capital of handmade crafts, sartorial swish, and once-in-a-lifetime finds.

E Marinella is a Chiaia institution for tie-making, and any trip to Naples should involve a coffee with owner Maurizio and a made-to-measure *cravatta*. (p84)

Head to Vietri sul Mare and visit **Ceramica Pinto** for a double dose of hand-painted majolica tile and local historical lore (both magical). (p134)

It might be sold worldwide but the flagship **Carthusia** store in Capri is an experience in itself, where flowers are always in bloom. (p112)

It's Christmas all year round on **Via San Gregorio Armeno** in Naples, where expert craftspeople sell handmade nativity figures with centuries of tradition behind them. (p30)

Almost anywhere you go in Sorrento you'll find inlaid wood masters plying their trade, but only **Mastellone** will let you take part. (p139)

THE BEST

Live Experiences

Nothing is quite like having a front-row seat, whether it's a musical festival, a championship game or a modern miracle. Luckily, Naples has it all.

The **Ravello Festival** is world famous for bringing musicians to this tiny hilltop town on the Amalfi Coast every year, and it's well worth planning your travel to be there for it. (p126)

Catch a football match at the **Stadio Diego Armando Maradona** and root for the home team along with tens of thousands of Neapolitans who are the biggest fans you'll ever meet. (pictured above left; p84)

Even if you're not a fan of opera, the gilded interiors of the **Teatro San Carlo** are the perfect backdrop for ballet, music and ensemble performances. (pictured above right; p60)

One of the biggest in Italy, **Napoli Pride** draws thousands of people to celebrate community and solidarity in Naples (along with fantastic music and tons of great food). (p25)

Three times a year, the **Duomo di Napoli** is abuzz with the Miracle of San Gennaro, a religious festival that makes believers of anyone who attends. (p38)

THE BEST

Archaeological Experiences

You know the big names, and they're just as impressive as you've heard. But don't sleep on the smaller spots because they've got centuries of treasures waiting to be discovered.

Dedicate a day to **Pompeii**, where you can even sign up to participate in excavations to be a part of history. (p90)

Seaside **Herculaneum** is bursting with incredible architecture, art and artefacts that have been unearthed over the centuries. (pictured above left; p98)

You don't have to leave the centre of Naples to see thousands of years of history – go underground at **Napoli Sotterranea** for a peek into the past. (pictured above right; p44)

The Ancient Greek **Ipogeo dei Cristallini** is one of the best-kept secrets in La Sanità, so grab your hard hat and have a look at one of the earliest traces of Naples. (p70)

Capri might be full of modern-day glam but the ruins at **Villa Jovis** are a glimpse into its ancient past, back when it was an emperor's paradise. (p108)

Right: Tempio di Apollo (p91), Pompeii

FROM LEFT: ALYSTA/SHUTTERSTOCK ©, PHOTONN/SHUTTERSTOCK ©, MARABELO/GETTY IMAGES ©

PLAN YOUR TRIP

THE BEST
Hiking Experiences

With a dramatic coastline and island cliffs, you're spoilt for choice on a hike, no matter what your fitness level is.

The iconic **Path of the Gods** (Sentiero degli Dei) is a challenging trek through the hinterlands of Amalfi, but well worth it for the views over the sea. (p122)

Hike to the top of the Amalfi Coast at **Santa Maria dei Monti** and gaze out over the entire peninsula, from Naples to Salerno. (p134)

See Capri from above at **Monte Solaro**, where the views are panoramic and if you need a hand, there's a cable car. (pictured above left; p113)

Punta Campanella is the closest point to Capri on the Sorrento Peninsula but it feels like you're just outside heaven. (p133)

The volcano might be sleeping now but **Mt Vesuvius** is alive with natural wonders that you'll catch on a hike up. (pictured above right; p96)

Right: The Path of the Gods (Sentiero degli Dei; p122)

FROM LEFT: WIRESTOCK/ISTOCK ©, VACLAV VOLRAB/SHUTTERSTOCK ©, TRABANTOS/SHUTTERSTOCK ©

PLAN YOUR TRIP

Bagni Regina Giovanna (p132)

THE BEST

Seaside Experiences

It's impossible to think about Naples without the sea, and there are an enormous range of spots for sun and swimming (sand optional).

Centuries of secret swimmers have found their bliss at **Bagni Regina Giovanna** in Sorrento, where protected pools make for idyllic paddling. (p132)

The **Grotta Azzurra** is hardly a secret, but time it right and you'll see the sapphire jewel of Capri in all its glory. (p112)

Get on board a traditional wooden boat in **Positano** and see the postcard city the way it's supposed to be seen, from the azure waters of the sea. (p130)

Grab a boat to tiny Procida and discover the **Spiaggia di Chiaia** beach, hiding in plain sight and welcoming locals to its tiny coves. (p117)

It may not be glam but **Mappatella Beach** in Naples is a city beach with lots of heart, and the perfect place for a midday swim. (p89)

Best for Kids

Take budding archaeologists to **Pompeii** for a day amongst the ruins, and let their imaginations run wild. (p90)

Herculaneum is manageable for families, stroller friendly, and an easy day trip from Naples for kids who love history. (p98)

Capri for kids might be a challenge but the sun shines bright in the **Giardini di Augusto**, where they can spot flowers in bloom. (p111)

Kids who like the spooky stuff will love the **Catacombe di San Gennaro**, where low-lit caves and lots of legends are better than any haunted house. (p70)

Street art is as much a part of Naples as pizza, so why not take the kids on a walking tour through some of the best-known spots? (Then, get some pizza.) (p56)

The historic **Ospedale delle Bambole** has been fixing dolls for centuries, and it'll bring a smile to anyone's face, regardless of their age. (p43)

Best for Free

Join the crowds at **Piazza Maradona** to celebrate the neverending legend of Diego Maradona, the football player turned prodigal son of the city. (p54)

Wander the alleys of the **Mercato di Porta Nolana** where you'll find everything from fresh fish to contraband cigarettes being hawked by Neapolitan experts. (p49)

Relax in the grass at **Palazzo Reale di Capodimonte**, the royal forest where kings, queens, and characters have admired views over Naples for a century. (p67)

Art is everywhere at the **Toledo Metro Station** in Naples, a spectacular mosaic-filled underground world that many have called the most beautiful station in the world. (p58)

Capri may cost a pretty penny but the views from **Punta di Tragara** are free, and more beautiful than any shop window on the island. (p111)

Three Perfect Days

Visit the patron saint(s) of Naples before heading out to explore the western Campi Flegrei, Mt Vesuvius, and the southern spine of the Sorrento Peninsula and the Amalfi Coast.

DAY ONE

Only Have One Day?

MORNING

Go for baroque in the **Centro Storico** (p35). Start at the **Duomo** (pictured above left; p38), home to the city's Patron Saint, Gennaro (and his magic blood), then to the **Cappella Sansevero** (p40) to see the magnificent *Cristo Velato*. Admire dazzling majolica mosaics at the **Complesso Monumentale di Santa Chiara** (p44) before stopping in at **'O Cuzzetiello** (p46) for a massive panino that will fuel you till sunset.

AFTERNOON

Wander the Quartieri Spagnoli looking for street art before finishing at **Piazza Maradona** (p54), the shrine to Naples' other saint, Diego Maradona.

EVENING

Get cocktails at **Ex Falegnameria** (p62) and dinner at **Trattoria da Nennella** (p61), where entertainment is included.

Piazza Maradona (p54)

DAY TWO

A Weekend Trip

MORNING

Explore the leafy grounds around the **Museo di Capodimonte** (p67) and on your way back down to Earth, pass through the mystical tunnels of the **Catacombe di San Gennaro** (p70) in La Sanità.

AFTERNOON

Get in line for the best pizza in town at **Concettina ai Tre Santi** (p72) and then walk it off between the mythical **Ipogeo dei Cristallini** (p70) and the vibrant **La Chiesa di Santa Maria Maddalena ai Cristallini** (p69) church, painted back to life by local artists.

EVENING

Drinks and tarot cards at **Malocchio** (p63) will quickly become a folklore-filled dinner at **O' Vascio** (p61), where Nunziata's *pasta e patate* (pasta and potatoes) will make you believe in magic.

DAY THREE

A Short Break

MORNING

Early bird it at **Bar Mexico** (p46) for coffee and **Sfogliatelle Attanasio** (p46) for a *sfogliatella* (*riccio,* always) to fuel a wander through **Mercato della Pignasecca** (p57). Watch old ladies haggle with fishmongers while eels wiggle in time.

AFTERNOON

Grab the best sandwich of your life from **Salumeria Malinconico** (p61) before visiting the imposing **Certosa e Museo di San Martino** (p74). Don't forget to soak up the panoramic views before returning to Earth.

EVENING

Take the **Salita del Petraio** (pictured above right; p74) down and enjoy a lazy stroll through Chiaia, where you can reward yourself with wines and bites at **L'Ebbrezza di Noè** (p86). Finish it off with freshly fried *graffe* (doughnuts) at **Chalet Ciro** (p89) along the Mergellina waterfront.

If You Have More Time

Start Saturday with an espresso at **Caffè Gambrinus** (p62) to fuel an early day in **Pompeii** (p90). Take your time, visit the recently excavated sites, and don't forget to use the amphitheatre entrance.

Stop for lunch at **Zi'Caterina** (p91) before returning to Napoli Centrale. You could walk through town but then you'd miss the artistic masterpiece of **Toledo Metro Station** (p58) on Line 1.

Get out and stroll towards **Galleria Umberto I** (p59) to visit **Mondadori** (p63), one of Italy's largest bookstores.

Rooftop spritzes at **Anthill Cocktail Bar & Tapas** (p63) lead to unforgettable seafood and wine at **CrudoRe** (p86), followed by a walk along the **Lungomare** (p85). After that, a nightcap at **Astronomia Bar Segreto** (p63) is the best way to finish up a perfect day on the bay.

Toledo Metro Station (p58)

A City Day Trip

The **Reggia di Caserta** (pictured above left; p102) is an architectural marvel and an easy day trip by train from Naples. Check out the massive central arcade, known as the Cannocchiale, the Throne Hall, and the dominating Alexander Hall, named for Alexander the Great.

The **Royal Park** includes elaborate fountains and the famous English Garden. The **Percorso Massonico** takes about two hours and is well worth doing.

Caserta is also home to two of the top ten pizzerias in the world. Choose from **I Masanielli di Francesco Martucci** (p103) or **Sasà Martucci I Masanielli** (p103) – yep, they're brothers. Talk about a Royal Family.

On a Rainy Day

When the skies darken overhead, go underground! Originally dug by the Ancient Greeks for material to build Neapolis in the 4th century BCE, the network of underground tunnels that make up **Napoli Sotterranea** (pictured above right; p44) were used as aqueducts that supplied water to the city and stretched for nearly 450km. A community organisation began securing the site for the public in the 1980s and now it's one of the city's most fascinating attractions. Not only is it a great way to shelter from rain, it's also a perfect place to escape the summer heat.

The **MANN** (p58) is the city's largest museum and another great spot to escape the rain. It houses the second-largest collection of Egyptian artifacts in Italy and Magna Graecia relics from Campania.

Get Prepared

BOOK AHEAD

Two months before Book your hotel and any cooking classes or guided hikes you plan to do in Capri or on the Amalfi Coast.

One month before Book travel on ferries (in the high season) and make reservations at starred restaurants, which will fill up fast.

One to two weeks before Email **E Marinella** (p84) to reserve a tour of the workshop, and finalise food tours or pizza classes in Naples.

Manners Matter

Almost all Italians will greet people when they enter and leave a shop or cafe – not doing so is considered impolite. Try a simple *'buongiorno'* when you arrive and a *'grazie'* upon departing, and you'll be shocked by how much people appreciate it. Likewise, saying 'please' (even in English) when ordering a coffee goes a long way.

Caffe Sospeso

Writer Luciano De Crescenzo wrote, 'When someone is happy in Naples, they pay for two coffees: one for themselves, and another for someone else. It's like offering a coffee to the rest of the world.' Paying a coffee forward is once again a tradition for a new generation of coffee drinkers. Try it out, you're almost guaranteed a smile.

Things to Know

Cappuccino The cappuccino is a breakfast beverage: common wisdom says that milk helps to jump-start the bowels, to put it bluntly. That's why it is absolutely not consumed after a meal and why you *will* get strange looks if you order it then.

Churches Most churches are active sites with services and masses taking place. If you want to visit one, make sure to cover your shoulders or carry a scarf that you can use as a shawl in a pinch. Naples is particularly devout and you may be refused entry if dressed inappropriately.

Don't touch There is no point, ever, where it is permitted to touch, hold, or *especially* write on any archaeological ruin. Graffiti might have been cool 2000 years ago in Pompeii, but your tag is most certainly not welcome. If caught, you'll pay a hefty fine.

Safety Naples is nowhere near as dangerous as it once was, but you should still exercise caution when walking in crowded streets or at night.

TIPPING

In Naples, small tips are appreciated but not expected. Once you get to Capri and parts of the coast, it may be more customary.

10%
Restaurants & cocktail bars

Unusual
Cafes & bars

10%
Taxis & private cars

Unusual
Hotel staff

DAILY BUDGET

BUDGET: Less than €100

- Double room in a budget hotel: **€50–110**
- Pizza or street food lunch/dinner: **€15**
- Bus, metro or funicular ticket: **€1.10**
- Return train ticket to Pompeii: **€5.60**
- Three-day Artecard pass: **€21**

MIDRANGE: €100–200

- Double room in a midrange hotel: **€140**
- Lunch and dinner in a local restaurant: **€25–50**
- Return express-train ticket to Pompeii: **€11**

TOP END: More than €200

- Double room in a four- or five-star hotel: **€150–450**
- Top restaurant dinner: **€50–120**
- Hydrofoil to Capri: **€21.50** (one-way)

Currency
Euro €

Language
Italian

Time
Central European Time CET (GMT+2)

ANDRZEJ GDULA/SOCIETÀ CAMPANA BENI CULTURALI ©

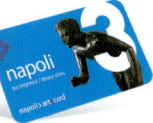

TIP

The Artecard is an amazing deal, with admission into museums as well as discounts on transport all over Naples. If you plan on being here more than one day, it's totally worth getting.

When to Go

There's never a bad time to visit Naples, but the sweet spot to hit the coast and islands takes a little planning.

Whatever time of year you visit Naples, there's always a full calendar of events on offer and you're highly likely to enjoy fine weather. That said, the summers get steamy so aim for the shoulder seasons, especially if you've got some flexibility for a city break.

The Amalfi Coast is tricky. Summers are critically crowded and prices soar, but most services close once the high season ends (they too need a break, after all). If May and June fit your calendar, you'll get ideal weather before temperatures (and tempers) start to rise.

Must-see Festivals

February–March During **Carnevale** in the lead-up to Easter, you'll see children dressed in costumes, confetti all over the street, and a bevy of delicious holiday sweets in shops, culminating in colourful float processions.

15 August The Catholic feast of the Assumption, **Ferragosto**, is one of Campania's most beloved (and wildest) celebrations. It's the apex of the summer season, and the most crowded. The parties, concerts and general mayhem are true to the holiday's pagan roots.

June–August Music lovers come from all over to attend **Ravello Festival** (p126) whose world-class events are often held in the beautiful Villa Rufolo's cascading gardens.

Late November–January Visit Salerno to see amazing *illuminari* (light installations) during **Le Luci d'Artista** turn the city into a Christmas wonderland.

Naples Weather

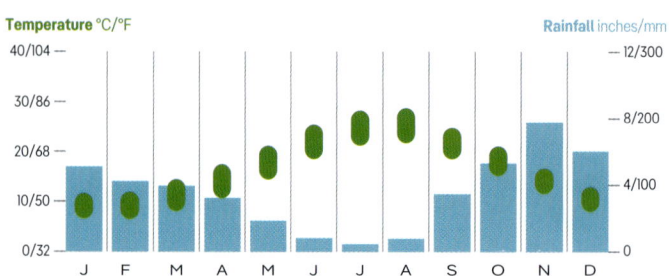

Ravello Festival (p126)

Local Highlights

June–July Like it does with everything else, Naples goes big with **Napoli Pride**. Expect cheeky art, street dancing, and a raucously fun atmosphere that everyone in the city enjoys.

July Notte delle Lampare is a historical re-enactment of Cetara's ancient anchovy-fishing technique of using a *lampara* (lamp) to attract fish to the water's surface, followed by anchovy tastings, concerts and fireworks.

September La Festa del Pesce on Fornillo beach takes place on the last Saturday of September and is the best way to experience Positano.

19 September Three times a year, an ampoule containing what's said to be the blood of Naples' patron saint undergoes a miraculous transformation from solid to liquid, if we're lucky. Head to the feast day, **Festa di San Gennaro** (p39), for the biggest parties and best weather.

THE REAL DEAL ON ACCOMMODATION

Holiday flats in Naples, Capri and the Amalfi Coast have artificially inflated the real estate market, meaning locals often can't afford to live in their hometowns. Hotels are prolific in the area and advance booking translates to great deals. Do you really need a kitchen?

✈ Getting There

Naples International Airport (Capodichino), 7km northeast of the city centre, is southern Italy's main airport. The city is also well connected by high-speed trains to all of Italy's other major cities.

From the Airport to the City Centre

By Bus
The Alibus airport shuttle connects the airport to Napoli Centrale (Piazza Garibaldi) and the Molo Angioino cruise-ship terminal, located beside the Molo Beverello fast-ferry and hydrofoil terminal. One-way tickets cost €5 and can be purchased on board. Buses run every 10 to 30 minutes.

By Taxi
Official taxi fares from the airport are as follows: €25 to Chiaia, Mergellina and Posillipo; €21 to Piazza Municipio or the Molo Beverello fast-ferry and hydrofoil terminal; and €18 to Napoli Centrale (Piazza Garibaldi) and the *centro storico*. Taxi companies include Consortaxi, Radio Taxi La Partenope and Taxi Napoli.

Car Hire
All major companies operate in Naples, but a word to the wise: driving in the city can be stressful and downright nerve-wracking along the coast. There are also rules against driving in city centres and exorbitant fees for parking. In short, you need that car less than you think you do.

Other Points of Entry

Train
The city's main train station is **Napoli Centrale**, just east of the *centro storico*. From here, the national rail company Trenitalia runs regular direct services to Rome (€13 to €48, 70 minutes to three hours, around 66 daily). High-speed private rail company Italo also runs daily direct services to Rome (€15 to €40, 70 minutes, around 20 daily). Most Italo services stop at Roma Termini and Roma Tiburtina stations and connect to all major Italian cities.

Sea
Slow ferries for Sicily, the Aeolian Islands and Sardinia sail from **Molo Angioino** and **Calata Porta di Massa**. Car ferries to Ischia and Procida also depart from Calata Porta di Massa. Both terminals are well connected to metro lines.

🚊 Getting Around

Naples has a well developed (and beautiful!) metro system, as well as funicular railways and an extensive bus network. As you go further south, you'll become fast frenemies with the Circumvesuviana train that runs to Sorrento and the SITA buses that cross the Amalfi Coast. Prepare for delays, but hey, the wait is lovely.

Metro

Like city buses, Metro Line 1 is operated by ANM. Trains run from Napoli Centrale (Garibaldi) to Vomero and the northern suburbs via the city centre. Metro Line 2 is operated by Italy's Ferrovie dello Stato (FS). Trains run from Gianturco to Napoli Centrale (Garibaldi) and on to Pozzuoli. Change for Line 1 at Garibaldi or Piazza Cavour (known as Museo on Line 1).

City Buses

Purchase your ticket at kiosks, tobacconists and vending machines and validate it in the machines on the bus. Increasingly more buses are equipped with Tap&Go, or purchase ANM tickets through the Unico App. There is no central station for city buses, but most pass through Piazza Garibaldi. Some city bus routes do not run on Sunday. A small number of routes run through the night, marked with an 'N' before their route number.

Funicular Trains

The four funicular (pictured) lines that connect residential hilltop neighbourhoods with the centre and seaside are also a great way to

FROM LEFT: NISSRINE MAHMOUD/SHUTTERSTOCK ©, GREG ELMS/LONELY PLANET ©

--- **ESSENTIAL APP** ---
Buy tickets for different transport companies in Naples and the coast through the UnicoCampania app or download the Artecard app – urban transport is included with museum entries.

snap photos of the coast and entertain kids. They're also wheelchair accessible and Tap&Go compatible.

Circumvesuviana

Circumvesuviana trains run from Napoli Porta Nolana to Sorrento but most people get on at **Napoli Centrale** (Garibaldi). Direct trains (D) arrive in Sorrento in 70 minutes from Naples but the faster 'Diretissimo' (DD) trains take 50 minutes. All trains stop at Herculaneum (Ercolano) and Pompeii (Villa dei Misteri).

SITA Buses

The SITA bus is the main form of transport between all 22 towns on the peninsula. Tickets can be purchased at tobacconists or through the Unico App, and some buses are equipped with Tap&Go. Be aware that they get particularly crowded from June through August. The buses share the SS163 with all the cars coming and going so expect delays and traffic jams.

Taxis & Rideshares

Official taxis are white and metered so make sure that the meter is running. Taxis can be exorbitant, especially once you're on the coast or islands. Make sure you confirm the rate beforehand if it's a longer distance: you'll usually be charged €1 per kilometre, there *and* back. Guide dogs and wheelchairs are carried free of charge. There are taxi stands at most of the city's main piazzas. Book a taxi by calling Consortaxi, Taxi Napoli or Radio Taxi La Partenope.

Uber and FreeNow are used in Naples but less so outside the city.

Public Transport Essentials

Digital Payments

Contactless payments (Tap&Go, app-based, e-ticket) are increasingly more commonplace around Campania but some lines, like the SITA bus, aren't yet equipped with the technology. To be safe, get paper tickets if you plan to be on the coast: you can get them just outside of the Sorrento EAV station, on your way to the bus stop.

Boats and Ferries

Naples, the islands and the Amalfi Coast are served by a comprehensive ferry network but it operates primarily between April and October. Catch fast ferries and hydrofoils for Capri, Sorrento, Ischia (both Ischia Porto and Forio) and Procida from Molo Beverello in front of Castel Nuovo. Ferries for the Amalfi Coast depart from Salerno Concordia and reach six of the coastal towns.

Accessible Travel

Many efforts are being made to make Naples more accessible. Wheelchair-friendly ramps, lifts and toilets are now common at museums and train stations. Some city buses have extra-large central doors, access ramps and a dedicated space for a wheelchair. Numerous hydrofoils and ferries are also wheelchair friendly. Some taxis are equipped to carry passengers in wheelchairs; ask for a taxi for a *sedia a rotelle* (wheelchair). Italy's national rail company, Trenitalia, offers a national helpline for passengers with a disability at 199 303060 (6.45am to 9.30pm).

TRAVEL COSTS

Train/bus ticket €1.10–4.50

Artecard Naples 3-day €27

Taxi, Napoli Centrale to Molo Beverello €16–20

ALWAYS TAP OUT!

To avoid a higher fare, make sure you tap your card upon exiting a train station or bus. Most stations have clearly indicated tap out points.

TICKETS

TIC (Ticket Integrato Campani) tickets are available at kiosks, tobacconists and vending machines. These are valid on all city metro (except line 2), bus and funicular services, including Circumvesuviana and Cumana trains within the Naples city zone. Unico Campania regulate a uniform fare system applicable to all local public transport in the city of Naples.

Ticket Type	Price	Validation Time
TIC biglietto integrato urbano	€1.60	90 minutes
TIC biglietto giornaliero integrato urbano	€4.50	until midnight
ANM – city buses, the four funiculars, and metro lines 1 and 6	€1.10	single-use ticket
Ferrovie dello Stato (FS) – metro line 2	€1.30	single-use ticket

🎁 A Few Surprises

Think you know Naples and the Amalfi Coast? There's always something new to discover, often hiding in plain sight.

Vintage Village

Via Mezzacannone has no fewer than 10 vintage stores in a square block, and many of them have been there in some form since the end of World War II. Browse the aisles with students, punks and fashion designers looking for a little inspiration.

The City of Bones

The creepy yet compelling **Cimitero delle Fontanelle** (p70) is home to centuries of unclaimed skeletons, and the Church of Santa Maria delle Anime in Purgatory in Arco, in the centre of Naples, is home to a cult that worships anonymous souls. Ready to get spooky?

Street Art Stories

Naples has always been an open-air museum but the proliferation of **street art** in the past few decades has given the city new life as a living work of art. Take a tour or walk through the city to see its history painted in brilliant colour strokes.

Everyday is Christmas

Also known as Via dei Presepi, **Via San Gregorio Armeno** is an open-air workshop making Christmas figurines (known as *pastori*) all year round. With more than 700 years of history behind them, craftspeople continue the tradition of moulding iconic figurines that find their way into nativity scenes worldwide.

Match of the Day

The SSC Napoli football (soccer) team is more than a sport for Neapolitans, it is a form of devotion. Head west to Fuorigrotta and join the faithful for a match at the **Stadio Diego Armando Maradona** (p84), a house of worship named for the legendary player who changed the game, and the city.

OFFBEAT NAPLES

Piazza Dante contains Europe's only **Equation Clock** (p59), which calculates the real-time when noon strikes, different every day.

Ospedale delle Bambole (p43) is a hospital for broken dolls and is alternatively cute and creepy, depending on who you ask.

La Chiesa di Santa Maria Maddalena ai Cristallini (p69) is a testament to the unique character of La Sanità neighbourhood.

Castel dell'Ovo (p85), Naples' iconic seaside castle, is actually one of Virgil's practical jokes.

Cimitero delle Fontanelle (p70)

Castel dell'Ovo (p85)

PLAN YOUR TRIP A FEW SURPRISES

Explore Naples & the Amalfi Coast

Centro Storico 35
Toledo & Quartieri Spagnoli 51
La Sanità & Capodimonte 65
Santa Lucia & Chiaia 77
Capri Town & the Isle of Capri 105
The Amalfi Coast & Sorrento Peninsula 119

Worth a Trip

Certosa e Museo di San Martino 74
Pompeii 90
Mount Vesuvius 96
Herculaneum (Ercolano) 98
Reggia di Caserta 102

Naples & the Amalfi Coast's Walking Tours

Walk Centro Storico 42
Walk Mercato & Borgo Orefici 48
Walk Quartieri Spagnoli 56
Walk the Holy Mile in Sanità 68
Walk Classical Chiaia 80
Walk a Sartorial Street Tour 82
Walk Mergellina 88
Walk the Arco Narturale 110
Walk Procida 116
Walk the Sorrento Centro Storico 128
Walk Positano at Sunrise 130

Quartieri Spagnoli (p56)
ARCADY/SHUTTERSTOCK ©

See p46 for eating, drinking and shopping listings

Explore
Centro Storico

The ancient centre of Naples tells the story of a city made in contrasts. The ancient Greek urban plan, known as the *decumani,* has become a well-trodden tourist path with plenty of kitschy 'Spaccanapoli' souvenirs but you'll also find revered monuments and timeless treasures. The magnificent Duomo arches towards the sky just as the narrow confines of Napoli Sotterranea snake underfoot, and the artistry of *pastori* (figurine makers) along Via San Gregorio Armeno spills out into prolific street art. Whether you're wandering through MADRE or studying the contours of *Cristo Velato,* art surrounds you in this part of the city. And when you get hungry you're spoilt for choice in a neighbourhood where tastiness is next to godliness, a feast for all senses.

Getting Around

 Train
Napoli Centrale is the main transit point for high-speed trains and city circulation, and it links lines that run throughout the region.

 Metro
Centro storico metro stations Dante, Museo, Università and Duomo on Line 1 and Piazza Cavour on Line 2.

 Bus
Route R2 runs along Corso Umberto I at the southern end of the neighbourhood, connecting Napoli Centrale to Piazza Trieste e Trento.

 Walk
The *centro storico* is best absorbed on foot, and the *decumani* (main streets) are largely given over to pedestrian traffic.

Duomo di Napoli (p38)
GIMAS/SHUTTERSTOCK ©

THE BEST

UNDERGROUND HISTORY
Napoli Sotterranea (p44)

JEWEL ENCRUSTED APOCALYPSE PREVENTION
Duomo di Napoli (p38)

STREET FOOD GREATEST HITS Antichissima Pizzeria Port'Alba 1738 (p46)

BEST MODERN ART
MADRE (p45)

LIFELIKE ARTWORK
Cappella Sansevero (p40)

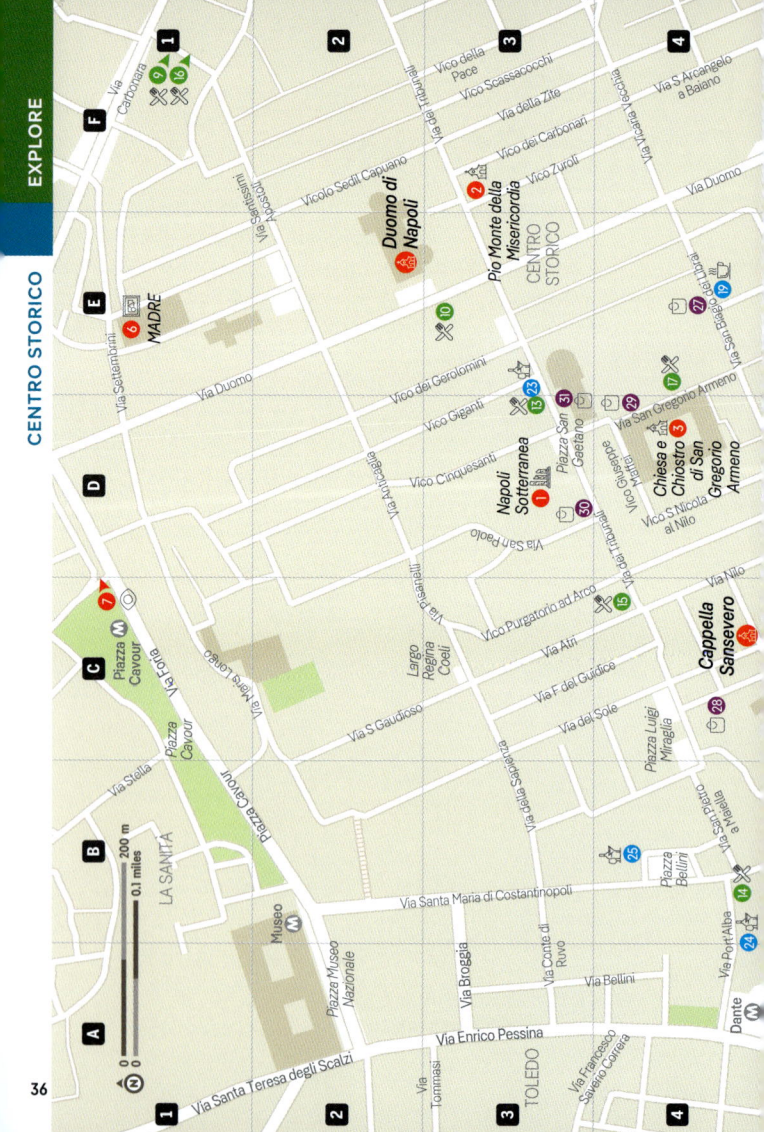

EXPLORE

CENTRO STORICO

For more see
- Top Experiences p38
- Experiences p44
- Eating p46
- Drinking p46
- Shopping p47

Key locations visible on map:
- Duomo
- Piazza Nicola Amore
- BORGO OREFICI
- Piazzetta del Nilo
- Piazza San Domenico Maggiore
- Chiesa del Gesù Nuovo
- Complesso Monumentale di Santa Chiara
- Piazza del Gesù Nuovo
- DANTE
- Piazza Dante
- Piazza Monteoliveto
- Piazza Carità
- Piazza Matteotti
- Università

Streets visible:
- Via dei Cimbri
- Via Museo Filangieri
- Via d'Afflitto
- Via Grande Archivio
- Via S Baldacchini
- Via Nuova Marina
- Via B Capasso
- Via Ernesto Capocci
- Vico S Severino
- Vico SS Filippo e Giacomo
- Via G Paladino
- Corso Umberto I
- Via Porta di Massa
- Via Alcide de Gasperi
- Via G C Cortese
- Via Marchese Campodisola
- Vico Donnaromita
- Via Mezzocannone
- Via Francesco de Sanctis
- Vico San Gerónimo
- Via San Giovanni Maggiore Pignatelli
- Via S Chiara
- Via Santa Chiara
- Via S Aspreno
- Via A Petroni
- Via G Sanfelice
- Vico San Domenico Maggiore
- Via Paladino Giovanni
- Via Benedetto Croce
- Via San Sebastiano
- Via del Gesù Nuovo
- Calata Trinità Maggiore
- Via Carrozzieri all'Posta
- Via Monteoliveto
- Via S Maria la Nova
- Via Cisterna dell'Olio
- Via S Anna dei Lombardi
- Via D Lioy
- Via T Senise
- Via T Caravita
- Via C Battisti
- Via Toledo

★ TOP EXPERIENCE

Duomo di Napoli

Like everything in Naples, the 13th century Gothic Duomo rests on layers of history. A late Imperial Roman aqueduct covers a stretch of Ancient Greek road, and it all guards the relics of patron saint San Gennaro, whose miraculous blood protects the city.

MAP P36 **E2**

PLANNING TIP
The museum is separate from the Duomo but can be accessed through the chapel if you buy your tickets online. If you're in town during one of the three festival days, expect big (jubilant) crowds.

Book your tickets for the museum here.

Cappella di San Gennaro

This show-stopping **chapel** (pictured) was designed to a Greek-cross plan by Theatine priest and architect Francesco Grimaldi, and completed in 1646. Cosimo Fanzago executed the entrance, statues and inlaid marble decoration, Jusepe de Ribera painted the nail-biting *St Gennaro Escaping the Furnace Unscathed* and Giovanni Lanfranco created the swirling dome fresco, *Paradise*. Hidden behind the altar is a 14th-century silver bust that stores two vials filled with the miraculously liquefying blood of the chapel's eponymous saint.

Museo del Tesoro

The **Museo del Tesoro di San Gennaro** *(Museum of the Treasure of San Gennaro; tesorosangennaro.it)* is adjacent to the chapel and leads to an underground maze of rooms. While 'treasures' usually indicate the relics of a saint, this collection of offerings rivals the Crown Jewels at Buckingham Palace in both splendour and value. Admission to the museum costs €15 and is organised in time slots. The museum also provides mobile phones with built-in audio guides for a €1 deposit – bring Bluetooth headphones with you to connect.

MARCOBRIVIO.GALLERY/SHUTTERSTOCK ©

The Miracle of San Gennaro

The blood of San Gennaro is said to have been saved by a devotee after his rather gruesome death in 305, and it has become famous for the liquefaction that occurs three times a year. On the first Saturday in May, 19 September and 16 December, thousands of faithful flock to the Duomo for this miraculous event. If the blood liquefies, the city is protected. If it doesn't, it signals imminent disaster including war, famine or disease. Before you laugh, consider that the blood of San Gennaro remained solid in 1939 (before WWII), 1980 (before a major earthquake) and 2020.

QUICK BREAK
For cheap, nourishing Neapolitan street food, stop at nearby **Antica Pizzeria Di Matteo** (p46).

★ TOP EXPERIENCE

Cappella Sansevero

This family chapel turned museum is a quick but impactful visit. The Rococo design houses almost 30 works of art, most notably the *Cristo Velato*, a marble statue so lifelike that it was believed to not even have come from human hands.

MAP P36 **C4**

PLANNING TIP
Even with tickets, you may be waiting in line to enter as the staff try to stagger entrances. Additionally, photos and video are prohibited in the chapel and the policy is strictly enforced.

Book your tickets here.

Cristo Velato

Giuseppe Sanmartino's deeply moving 1753 **sculpture of Christ** (pictured) lies under a marble veil so thin that many have wondered whether the chapel's alchemist patron, Prince Raimondo di Sangro, managed to transform cloth into stone. Magical or not, the sculpture is extraordinary and one which led the revered neoclassical sculptor Antonio Canova to dramatically declare that he would have given up 10 years of his own life to produce such a masterpiece.

It's one of several artistic wonders that include Francesco Queirolo's sculpture *Disinganno* (Disillusion) and Antonio Corradini's *Pudicizia* (Modesty).

Chapel Frescoes

Francesco Maria Russo's lavish *Gloria del Paradiso* (Glory of Heaven) colours the ceiling but Di Sangro was so unimpressed with the fresco that he willed his eldest son to have it redone, an order which was thankfully ignored. Ironically, the prince himself formulated the vibrant colours that Russo used, which have kept their intensity since its completion in 1749.

Secret Chambers

Beneath the chapel, Di Sangro's secret chamber houses a pair of meticulously preserved human

MARCOBRIVIO.PHOTO/SHUTTERSTOCK ©

arterial systems, one male, the other female. Rumours have surrounded the figures for centuries, but the prince was no stranger to wild neighbourhood gossip – to many locals, the inventor and Freemason was seen as a local Dr Faustus, a man who had made a pact with the devil to dabble in magic. Debate still circles the models: are the arterial systems real or reproductions? And if they are real, just how was such an incredible state of preservation achieved? More than two centuries on, the mystery surrounding the alchemist prince and his abilities lives on.

QUICK BREAK
For interesting wines and charcuterie, graze piazza-side at nearby **Jamón** (p47). Lunch or dinner, tuck into flavour-packed Neapolitan *ragù* at **Tandem** (p46).

WALKING TOUR

Walk Centro Storico

Vespas buzz, locals passionately debate, and all of it echoes off the narrow alleyways framed by ancient buildings. Soak it all up and mix it with the ever-present aroma of a perfect *ragù napoletana* simmering in a secret kitchen, and you'll know that you couldn't be anywhere else in the world except in the heart of Naples.

START	END	LENGTH
Piazza del Gesù Nuovo	Piazza Bellini	2km; 2½ hours

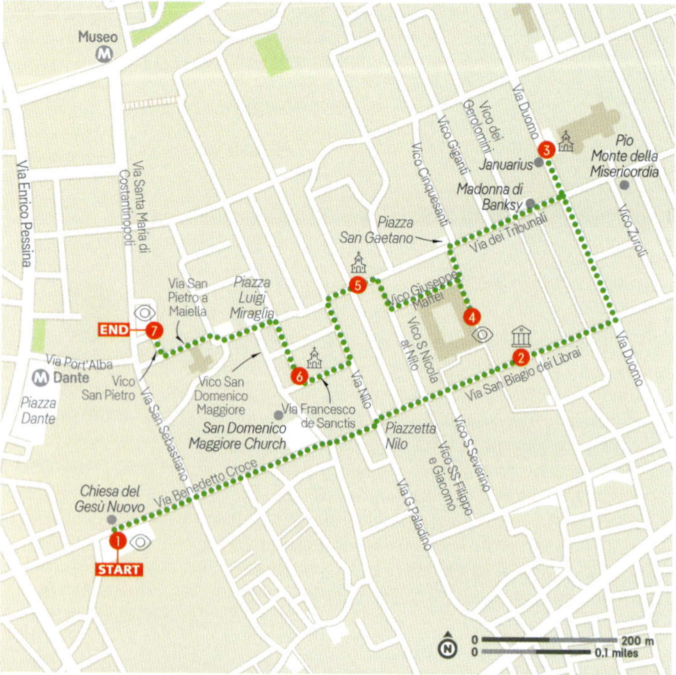

1 Historic Piazza

Start at **Piazza del Gesù Nuovo** in front of the diamond-studded Chiesa del Gesù Nuovo, with centuries of history including WWII bomb remnants. Spaccanapoli, the main drag, runs through here towards Piazzetta Nilo where the frescoes of the San Domenico Maggiore church peek out of ceremonial doors.

2 An Eerie Alleyway

Follow the handwritten signs toward the **Ospedale delle Bambole**, a 200-year-old doll hospital that's become a social media mainstay but remains a slightly creepy yet strangely endearing place, fitting with the eerie mood of the alleyways in Naples.

3 Saintly Stops

From there, head to the Decumano Maggiore via Pio Monte della Misericordia for Caravaggio, and then make your way to the **Duomo** (p38). Once you've made a wish to San Gennaro, stop into his namesake restaurant/bottega, Januarius (p46), where the food is as miraculous as the saint.

4 Christmas Everyday

Once suitably sated, continue on Via dei Tribunali and do a sign of the cross at the Madonna di Banksy, graffiti left by the anonymous street artist. Follow the crowds to **Via San Gregorio Armeno**, the little alley bursting with lively nativity scenes every day of the year.

5 Creepy Churches

The creepy yet alluring Purgatorio ad Arco is the home of the Pulcinella statue, whose nose is said to bring good luck if you rub it. The cultish church of **Santa Maria delle Anime** just beyond it adopts unknown human remains and the underground church is one of the most haunting sites in the city. The sacred and profane play catch with each other in Naples, and it's here you'll realise that you're the ball.

6 Veiled Wonders

Shake off the shivers and pass through the **Cappella Sansevero** (p40) where the gleaming marble of *Cristo Velato* is so lifelike, you'll swear you can see the figures breathing. From every angle, you'll be enchanted.

7 Chill with a Spritz

Come to your senses in the raucous **Piazza Bellini** where Greek walls still hug the corners and students converge to shake off their demons. This kind of revelry tends to evoke the ghosts of the past and in a city like Naples, there are plenty to rouse.

EXPERIENCES

Dig Through Ancient Layers
ARCHAEOLOGICAL SITE

MAP: ① P36 **D3**

Spend a couple of hours exploring **Napoli Sotterranea** *(napoli sotterranea.org; adult/child €15/8)*, a 450km network originally dug by the Ancient Greeks for material to build Neapolis in the 4th century BCE. The Romans later used these underground tunnels as aqueducts and in WWII, more than 200,000 Neapolitans were saved by seeking refuge here. This vast maze was forgotten until a community organisation began restoring them for public use in the 1980s. Now it's one of the most popular experiences in the *centro storico* but well-organised guided tours keep it from ever getting (or feeling) overcrowded.

Don't miss the **Hypogeum Gardens**, a 35m-deep nursery that was born from an experiment at the 2015 Expo on alternative growing atmospheres. It's almost surreal to be greeted by verdant plant life amid an ancient cave complex, and it is strikingly beautiful.

The tour goes through some narrow spaces and some of the passageways are dimly lit, but if you truly want to know Naples, start from below.

Explore Historical Churches
CHURCHES

Not minor in any way, the many churches in the *centro storico* each have an incredible wealth of history and art to share. Whenever possible, try to duck in to see some of the sights for yourself.

The **Pio Monte della Misericordia** (MAP: ② P36 **F3**) charity guard Caravaggio's *Sette Opere della Misericordia* in an octagonal, 17th-century church. The frescoes in the **Chiesa e Chiostro di San Gregorio Armeno** (MAP: ③ P36 **D4**) are one of the best examples of Luca Giordano's intricate work in central Naples (which is saying quite a lot).

The **Chiesa del Gesù Nuovo** (MAP: ④ P36 **B6**) is also one of the best baroque examples in Naples and oozes Luca Giordano and Cosimo Fanzago. But for an explosion of colour, light and artistry don't miss the **Complesso Monumentale di Santa Chiara** (MAP: ⑤ P36 **B6**),

---

 **UNAUTHORIZED NAPLES**

If you see a distinctive 'Napoli' stencil on the streets, get your camera out. Two local artists, Zeal Off and They Lived, painted the stencil as a tribute to John McConnell, the graphic designer who originally submitted the work in 1985. The simple graphic tells the story of a place that teeters but remains unbreakable, and it has become a symbol of resilience and creative expression. The street art project is called 'Unauthorized Naples' and there are more than 30 stencils citywide.

an oasis of hand-painted majolica ceramic tilework set over 72 octagonal columns that connect to similarly decorated benches framing a lush private garden.

Observe Stories of the Streets STREET ART TOUR

The proliferation of street art in the past few decades has given Naples new life as a living work of art. Gennaro Cedrangolo, artist and founder of '400ml', a non-profit organisation dedicated to preserving street art in Naples, shows the city with different eyes on his **Napoli Paint Stories tour** *(instagram.com/napolipaintstories_tour, from €35)*. Here, street art is more than resistance: it's a kind of communion with the place itself, an offering to the delicate membranes of peeling facades that make Naples simultaneously vulnerable and mighty. Once again, the city will surprise you.

Gennaro offers tours around the entire city but his walk through the centre is a great intro to the street art of Naples. Tours of the centre feature artists including Diego Miedo, Blu, Cyop&Kaf, and Trallallà. There are also touching tributes to the city like *A New Parthenope* by Francisco Bosoletti. And of course, plenty of stories.

Feel Modern Art Moods MUSEUM

MAP: 6 P36 E1

Naples isn't all occultism and iconography: the museum of modern and contemporary art known as

REAL ALBERGO DEI POVERI
The **Real Albergo dei Poveri** (MAP: 7 P36 C1) or Palazzo Fuga as it's sometimes known, was an Enlightenment-era project designed to help the poor with housing, education and work. The largest palace in Naples, it has been a refuge for orphans, a trade school, and a juvenile court. Because of its protected status, restoration and repairs are complicated, and the task of preserving it gets ever more difficult. However, it is often the site of film festivals and cultural conferences, and has become the base for Napoli Pride Week. Whatever its future, the Real Albergo is part of the everlasting fabric of the city.

MADRE *(madrenapoli.it; adult/reduced €8/4)* is home to a powerhouse collection worth dedicating half a day to. In the lobby, French conceptual artist Daniel Buren sets the mood with his playful, mirror-panelled installation *Work in Situ*, with other specially commissioned installations from heavyweights like Anish Kapoor, Rebecca Horn and Sol LeWitt on level one. Level two houses the bulk of MADRE's permanent collection of painting, sculpture, photography and installations from other prolific 20th- and 21st-century artists, designers and architects.

LISTINGS

Best Places for...

€ Budget €€ Midrange €€€ Top End

See p36 for map of locations

Eating

Street Food

Tandem €
8 D5
For those who worship at the altar of *ragù*, this is your go-to spot. *12.30-3.30pm & 7-11.30pm*

'O Cuzzetiello €
9 F1
Unmissable and overflowing panini that will satisfy every craving you've ever had and fill you up until the next round. *11.30am-3.30pm, 7-11pm*

Sit-down Meals

Januarius €€€
10 E3
The cuisine is classical Neapolitan with down-to-earth products but the fresco ceilings are out of this world. *1-3pm, 7.30-11pm Wed-Mon*

La Locanda Gesù Vecchio €€
11 D6
Looking for a meal in a family home but haven't been adopted yet? This is the next best thing. *12-3.30pm & 7-11pm Tue-Sun*

Aria €€€
12 C8
This intimate Michelin-star restaurant proves that there's more to street food in Naples without ever looking down on it. *7.30-11pm Mon-Sat*

Pizza

Antica Pizzeria Di Matteo €€
13 D3
It's an obligatory stop for a reason; get there early and get it to go for a night out Naples style. *10am-midnight Mon-Sat, 10.30am-3pm Sun*

Antichissima Pizzeria Port'Alba 1738 €€
14 B4
Stellar pizzas, or go the tasting menu of *'Gli sfizi di Gennaro Luciano'*, a greatest hits of Neapolitan street food. *12-4.30pm & 6.30pm-midnight Wed-Mon*

Gino Sorbillo Antica Pizzeria €€
15 C4
While debate may rage over whether Gino Sorbillo's pizzas are the best in town, there's no doubt that the giant, wood-fired discs are a work of art. *noon-3.30pm & 7-11.30pm Mon-Sat*

Pastries

Sfogliatelle Attanasio €
16 F1
It might be the first you eat but you'll have a hard time topping this spot near the Central Station. *6.30am-7.30pm Tue-Sun*

Sfogliate e Sfogliatelle €
17 E4
Fight with whomever tells you that this isn't the reigning queen of the clamshell, because it's beyond dispute. *9am-7pm*

Drinking

Coffee

Bar Mexico
18 D8
This 1960s relic in Piazza Garibaldi serves a thick, sugary rocket fuel to remind you why you're here. *5.30am-8pm Mon-Sat*

Caffè Ciorfito
 E4

Right in the thick of it, this tried-and-true spot opens early and makes the perfect stop after nativity scene shopping. *6am-8pm Mon-Sat*

Bar Nilo
 D5

Is that really a lock of Maradona's hair in that frame? Best not to question it, especially when the espresso is this good. *7.30am-8pm Mon-Sat*

Cuccuma Caffè
 C5

The only place in the city to have a brew from the traditional flip pot, and some fine foods on offer to boot. *11.30am-10pm*

Cocktails

Jamón
 C5

Deli–wine bar at the top of Piazza San Domenico Maggiore with niche charcuterie and cheese offerings and the perfect *aperitivo* vibe after a hard day soaking up history. *10am-midnight*

Cantina Central 92
 E3

Opt for the quick (but tasty) drinks being sold at the door and select from an impressive wine list. *12.15-3.15pm Mon-Sat*

Libreria Berisio
 B4

Cosy atmospheric bookshop with a terrific cafe-bar open till the wee hours for craft cocktails and classics. *hours vary*

Spazio Nea
 B4

An art gallery and *aperitivo* spot on Piazza Bellini with charm in spades and drinks to match. *9am-2am, to 3am Fri & Sat*

Shopping

Made in Campania

Scriptura
 B5

This family-run boutique is a must for artisanal leather goods made using high-quality Campanian leather ranging from bags to belts and everything in between. *10am-8pm Mon-Sat*

Materia Mediterranea
 E4

A stylish boutique run by five young Neapolitan designers who draw inspiration from the city's colourful culture and history, making it the best spot for a unique gift. *10am-8pm Mon-Sat*

Bottega 21
 C4

Tuscan leather and Neapolitan creativity mean clean, simple designs for bags, wallets, belts, gloves, and notebook covers. *9.30am-8pm Mon-Sat*

Nativity Scenes

Ferrigno
 D4

King of the Christmas nativity scenes, Ferrigno's terracotta figurines are sought by collectors worldwide. *10.30am-1pm & 2-7pm Mon & Tue, 9.30am-7pm Wed-Sat*

La Scarabattola
30 D3

Handmade sculptures of *magi* (wise men), devils, and Neapolitan folk figures beloved by fashion designer Stefano Gabbana and Spanish royalty. *10.30am-2pm & 3.30-7.30pm Mon-Fri, 10am-8pm Sat*

Ars Neapolitana
31 D3

Drop into this workshop and you'll probably find Guglielmo sculpting or painting one of his impressively detailed terracotta saints, angels or 18th-century folkloric characters. *10am-7pm Mon-Sat*

Walk Mercato & Borgo Orefici

Dwarfed by the colossus of Piazza Garibaldi, the tract between Corso Umberto I and the port is a labyrinth of ancient streets full of intrigue, myth and vibrating street life. Dive into souk-like market stalls, seek out legend-laced churches, and haggle with heirloom businesses peddling everything from jewellery to coveted fabrics.

START	END	LENGTH
Mercato di Porta Nolana	Piazza Orefici	1.5km; one hour

1. Faith, Hope and Fish

The two towers on the medieval gate for which **Mercato di Porta Nolana** is named are called Faith and Hope, emblems of a city that relies heavily on both. Vendors peddle fish, vegetables, cheeses and more, speaking entirely in Neapolitan, until grannies buy them out at around 2pm, so get there early.

2. Miraculous Madonnas

The **Chiesa di Santa Maria del Carmine** is the hub for July's Festa della Madonna del Carmine, when fireworks mimic the blaze of the campanile (bell tower), said to be miraculously extinguished by the Madonna della Bruna. Look for the 13th-century Byzantine icon of the heavenly firefighter in the church's 16th-century tabernacle.

3. Revolutionary Piazza (and Pizza)

The imposing **Piazza Mercato** may look downtrodden but it's one of the city's most storied squares. The revolutionary Masaniello began his assault here, public executions used to take place here, and in a tonal shift, it's also the site of a huge Christmas market every year. Digest it all at Bro Ciro e Antonio Tutino, one of the best pizzerias in the city.

4. The Shifty Duke

Legend has it that the stone heads over the arch of 13th-century **Chiesa di Sant'Eligio Maggiore** represent Duke Antonello Caracciolo and maiden Irene Malarbi. Having traded her virture with Caracciolo to free her wrongfully imprisoned father, Isabella of Aragon forced the duke to marry Malarbi as punishment (ouch) before having him executed (bigger ouch).

5. (Not so) Beautiful Busts

Dip into Romanesque **Chiesa di San Giovanni a Mare** to catch of copy of the Donna Marianna, an ancient Greek bust whose shape inspired the Neapolitan saying *"Me pare Donna Marianna, 'a Capa 'e Napule'"*. For the uninitiated, that's an unattractive woman with a large head.

6. Dress it Up

Located in Naples' garment district, family-run **Fratelli D'Angelo di Donato** is a go-to for Neapolitan tailors and brides-to-be. In business since 1931, its shelves are a library of fabrics, from prestigious Taroni silk from northern Italy to collectable vintage fabrics from Versace.

7. Golden Days

The labyrinthine streets of the Borgo Orefici have housed Naples' most important goldsmiths, silversmiths and jewellers since medieval times. The four Consuls of the Goldsmiths' Guild supervised the district's craftsmen from **Piazzetta Orefici**, and the precious statues of the treasure of San Gennaro were formed and created here.

See p61 for eating, drinking and shopping listings

Explore
Toledo & Quartieri Spagnoli

Known as the Via Roma until 1980, the Via Toledo was an essential stop on the Grand Tour, with writers such as Stendhal writing paeans to the beauty of Naples after seeing it. Today, it is the commercial artery that runs through the city.

For centuries, the Quartieri Spagnoli was a forbidding, sinister place. But the stranglehold of criminality has finally been lifted and it's become one of the most visited parts of Naples. The contrast between Toledo and the Spagnoli remains but it is harmonious and compelling. This is where the soul of Naples lives.

Getting Around

 Metro
The Toledo Metro Station is an attraction unto itself and useful for getting to other parts of the city, as it's on the central Line 1.

 Funicular
The funicular station to Vomero is tucked away near Montesanto, connecting the hills to the centre of town.

 Walk
There's no better way to explore the entire area than on foot, whether you're window shopping or urban exploring.

THE BEST

STREET ART Murales in Piazza Maradona (p54)

EPIC HISTORY MUSEUM MANN (p58)

GLORIOUS SHOPPING Galleria Umberto I (p59)

OPEN-AIR LIVING ROOM Piazza Dante (p58)

OPULENT MUSEUM Palazzo Reale (p55)

Galleria Umberto I (p59)
PAGE FREDERIQUE/SHUTTERSTOCK ©

TOLEDO & QUARTIERI SPAGNOLI

TOLEDO & QUARTIERI SPAGNOLI

EXPLORE

For more see
- Top Experiences p54
- Experiences p58
- Eating p61
- Drinking p62
- Shopping p63

Key locations visible on map:
- Piazza Maradona
- Toledo Metro Station
- Galleria Umberto I
- Teatro San Carlo
- Palazzo Reale
- Piazza del Plebiscito
- Basilica di San Francesco di Paola
- Molo Angioino
- Porto Immacolatella
- Funicolare Centrale
- Parco Castello
- QUARTIERI SPAGNOLI
- Chiaia-Monte di Dio
- Largo San Martino

53

⭐ TOP EXPERIENCE

Piazza Maradona

You don't have to be a football fan to appreciate Piazza Maradona, although don't be surprised if you've become one by the time you leave. Now the most popular attraction in Naples, this impromptu shrine on Largo Emanuele de Deo has become larger than life.

MAP P52 **C6**

PLANNING TIP
On days when SSC Napoli plays, expect larger crowds than usual. If they win, it's a party. If they lose, the mood might be a bit sombre.

TRANSPORT
Take the 1 line to Toledo, or the 2 line to Montesanto. It's a short walk to Largo Emanuele de Deo from either.

The Piazza

When Argentinian football player Diego Maradona came to Naples in 1984, a small club became an international powerhouse. By 1986 the team had won the 'Scudetto' or series A title, a huge milestone for such an upstart team. After the second 'scudetto' in 1989, an enormous mural of Maradona was painted in the Quartieri Spagnoli, leading to the Largo Emanuele de Deo becoming informally known as Piazza Maradona. When Maradona died in 2020, citizens began to spontaneously flock to the square to leave offerings and it morphed into a pilgrimage site.

The Murals

The original Maradona mural draws street artists and soccer fans, but the square is filled with incredible street art. To see Francisco Bosoletti's *Pudicizia* 'in positive' you'll need to look through the negative filter on your camera. The Largo degli Artisti (Artists' Square), features three of the city's most famous artists: Totò, Massimo Troisi and Pino Daniele.

The Vibe

The Quartieri Spagnoli was a no-go zone for many years, but development and a reduction in organised crime has opened it to the world. When SSC Napoli won its third 'scudetto' in 2023, Piazza Maradona became the epicentre of celebrations that haven't stopped since and show no signs of slowing down.

TOP EXPERIENCE

Palazzo Reale

Palazzo Reale was conceived as a residence for Spain's King Philip III by the Bourbons during their rule of the Kingdom of Naples. Today it's a spectacular combination of art gallery, library and architectural masterpiece that shows just how good it is to be the king.

MAP P52 **D8**

Architectural Highlights

The palace was originally designed by late-Renaissance architect Domenico Fontana, with the oldest facade facing Piazza del Plebiscito. Make time to see the opulent marble scalone d'onore staircase, the gilt and marble **Royal Chapel**, and pay attention to the niches along the lower level, which hold statues of former rulers.

Opulent Interiors and Artworks

The Teatrino di Corte, a private theatre created by Ferdinando Fuga in 1768, is incredible. Other highlights include late-baroque artist Francesco De Mura's ceiling fresco in Room II and his canvas *Adoration of Shepherds* in Room IV. The Royal Chapel houses an 18th-century *presepe napoletano* (Neapolitan nativity scene) contributed to by Giuseppe Sanmartino, creator of the *Cristo Velato* sculpture in Naples' Cappella Sansevero.

Biblioteca Nazionale

Italy's third-largest library was inaugurated by Ferdinand IV in 1804 as the Royal Library of Naples, and its vaulted main **Reading Room** is breathtaking. You'll find a 17th-century globe in the library's Executive Offices section, and extraordinary carved-timber interiors in the Biblioteca Lucchesi Palli on the 2nd floor. Email a month ahead to view its ancient papyri, retrieved from Herculaneum.

PLANNING TIP

Theatre and opera fans can buy the combination ticket (€12) for entry to both the Palazzo Reale and adjoining MeMus theatre museum.

Scan for practical information.

Walk Quartieri Spagnoli

Once a no-go zone in central Naples, the Quartieri Spagnoli has become one of the most vibrant neighbourhoods in the city. Narrow streets crisscrossed with laundry lines and covered in street art mingle with the aromas of regional classics coming from restaurants tucked into tiny corners. It's the perfect place to wander.

START	END	LENGTH
Via Portamedina	Piazza Maradona	2km; two hours

1 Entering the Quartieri

Start at the **Ricordo Di Mattia Fagnoni Mural** on Via Portamedina, dedicated to a neighbourhood boy who died from a rare blood disease and painted by celebrated artist David Vecchiato. Pick your panini at Con Mollica o Senza, the legendary deli where sandwiches are colossal endeavours.

2 Where Local Grannies Haggle

Run the gauntlet at **Mercato della Pignasecca** where old-school fishmongers haggle with grannies and the scent of freshly fried calamari may lead you to make impulsive decisions. Don't miss the Murales alla Tarantina, dedicated to the *femminiello* (trans performer) who inspired Fellini.

3 Legendary Street Artists

Walk along **Vico Lungo del Gelso** where some of the over 200 graffiti pieces by local artists (and legends) Cyop&Kaf line the streets, recognisable by their primary colours and whimsical, geometrical shapes. The Piazza Figurella di Montecalvario bursts with artwork and sculpture and is a fine place to stop for no-frills cocktails at Spritz e Baracche.

4 Patron Saint Totò

Although his face is everywhere, **Vico Totò** is more than just an homage to the Italian actor Totò: the many arrows and drawings are the work of a neurodivergent children's collective in the Quartieri. This colourful street has become a focal point for the neighbourhood, not only for its art but for the inspiring stories behind them.

5 The Street Art Party

Along **Via Emanuele de Deo** you'll see more work from Cyop&Kaf, homages to Lucio Dalla, Totò, and Pino Daniele, and impromptu designs celebrating local jokes. And the atmosphere can become even more festive: the streets draped in celebration with the signature sky blue of SSC Napoli.

6 Honour Revolutionary Women

Head for the **Eleonora Pimentel Fonseca Mural**, which commemorates the poet and revolutionary who took part in the Jacobin movement in Naples. Executed by artist Leticia Mandragora, this 2019 work heralded the changing air in the Quartieri, as it revitalised an abandoned square.

7 The House that Maradona Built

The party peaks at **Piazza Maradona** (p54) and the spontaneous shrine to the patron saint of the Quartieri Spagnoli, Diego Maradona. Grab a blue spritz from La Bodega de D10s, and catch a glimpse of owner Don Antonio, who was the driving force behind the creation of this impromptu holy place.

EXPERIENCES

Get Lost in History at the MANN
MUSEUM

MAP: ① P52 D1

The **MANN** (*Museo Archaeologico Nazionale di Napoli; mann-napoli.it; €22*) is the largest museum in central Naples and you could easily spend a half day here.

The vast collection of Greek and Roman antiquities is part of the Farnese Collection of gems and marbles. There is also a trove of Roman bronzes as well as mosaics recovered from the ruins of Herculaneum and Pompeii. The Secret Room houses over 250 pieces of erotica, primarily from the two ancient cities, and were collected by the Bourbon monarchy. Over the centuries this room has been censored and celebrated, and always fascinating.

The MANN houses the second-largest collection of Egyptian artefacts in Italy, filling seven rooms and spanning six centuries. The impressive exhibition of Magna Graecia artefacts from all over Campania is also well worth a look.

Tickets are valid for two days. A separate ticket is required for the Magna Graecia collection (€1.50); entries are timed and you must wear shoe coverings.

Explore the Universe of Toledo Metro
ART/TRANSPORT

MAP: ② P52 D5

The **Toledo Metro Station** (*metroart.anm.it/stazioni-arte/toledo*) is often called the world's most beautiful station, and there's a good reason why. The crown jewel of the Stazione dell'Arte project is on Line 1 and has been open since 2012, connecting Via Toledo to both Vomero and the Port.

The photos you'll have seen don't do justice to the experience of walking through this dreamlike space. The Crater de Luz, a large cone that cuts through all the levels of the station designed by Oscar Tusquets Blanca, interacts with Robert Wilson's *Relative Light,* a symphony of 144 LED lights in a palette of luminous blues. As you descend below sea level, you're greeted by Olas, another work from Tusquets Blanca which covers the monumental hall in intense blue mosaics.

The metro operates from 6.20am to 11pm Thursday to Sunday and until 1.30am Friday and Saturday. Purchase tickets at the station or through the Unico app.

Stop Time in Piazza Dante
PUBLIC SQUARE

MAP: ③ P52 D3

What is now **Piazza Dante** was once Mercatello, the city's second-largest market. When the plague wiped out half of the city's population in 1656, however, the market stalls were traded in for burial pits until the bodies could be moved to the caves of the Fontanelle Cemetery.

The Vanvitelli-designed square, originally meant to honor Charles III, was instead named Piazza Dante to honour the poet whose statue sits in the centre. The piazza has become the living room of Naples, with used bookstores and cafes filled with people mixing, drinking, studying, or falling in love. Stop for a drink and don't be surprised if you stay all day.

Piazza Dante is also home to the only **Equation Clock** in Europe, an oddity worth noticing. Look up at the main clocktower and you'll see another, smaller one underneath. This clock calculates the real-time when noon strikes, which is different every day (sometimes by as much as 15 minutes). Leave it to Naples to bend the rules.

UNDERGROUND ART TOURS

Toledo station is part of a city-wide project called Stazione dell'Arte (Art Stations), which has transformed 12 stations along lines 1 and 6 into open-air museums, with more than 250 works of art on display from 90 international artists. Metro Art ANM's educational service promotes the Stazione dell'Arte with guided tours from trained art historians and engineers, and you can join a group or schedule a private tour. Check out metroart.anm.it for more information on booking as well as an ever-evolving list of new projects.

Channel Your Inner Flaneur   SHOPPING ARCADE
MAP: ④ P52 **D7**

If you think you've fallen asleep and woken up in Milan's Galleria Vittorio Emanuele, don't worry. You're just in Naples' most famous 19th-century arcade, built as an homage to its northern cousin, where you can happily spend a few hours.

Though the **Galleria Umberto I** was a UNESCO heritage site for decades, it was sadly neglected – neighbourhood kids used to play soccer games here. But it's been restored to its former glory and its four long halls extend magnificently out from the centre, forming an enormous cross that's visible from the hills above the city.

Walk through for an hour arm in arm with someone you just realised you love and then go spend time browsing the floor-to-ceiling bookshelves in the grand Mondadori (p63) that's just opened in the Galleria. Or grab a coffee and listen to the gentle tapping of feet on marble floors to feed your inner flaneur. If it's all a dream, there's no rush to wake up.

Hang out in the People's Square   PUBLIC MONUMENT
Piazza del Plebiscito (MAP: ⑤ P52 **D8**) is just opposite the Palazzo Reale (p55), framed by the

neoclassical **Basilica di San Francesco di Paola** (MAP: 6 P52 C8). The 19th-century architecture features a semicircular colonnade that hugs the vast commons and is topped by a Pantheon-like dome. The steps have become an iconic hangout in Naples, so save an evening for it.

Legend has it that Queen Margherita of Savoy would pardon any prisoner sentenced to death who could cross the vast expanse of the piazza. The catch? They had to be blindfolded.

No one ever managed to escape execution due to a curse cast by the queen to mock her prisoners, which says a lot about the world before reality TV. But since then, Neapolitans and tourists alike continue to attempt the feat, closing their eyes and attempting to walk the 170m (560ft) necessary to cross the exact centre of the square without running into one of its statues. Since the piazza has become pedestrian-only, it's a lot less death defying.

Enjoy a Night at the Opera
MUSIC/THEATRE

MAP: 7 P52 **D7**

Built in 1737, **Teatro San Carlo** (*teatrosancarlo.it; guided tours €9*) is the oldest continuously operating opera house in Europe. The current building is a replica of the original, which was destroyed by a fire in 1816. However, Antonio Niccolini's refit was so successful that no less a critic than Stendhal reported that it 'enraptured the soul'.

If you're an opera buff, this is a must do. The website offers a full schedule of performances and there are also classical concerts, ballet, and Christmas performances.

Even if *La Traviata* isn't quite your bag, San Carlo offers guided tours that take you beyond the opulent red and gold rotunda into a gilded world that will leave you speechless. Tours usually take in the foyers, elegant main hall and royal box (the best seat in the house) and tour tickets can be purchased at the theatre up to 15 minutes before each tour begins.

 RESISTING POVERTY TOURISM

The Quartieri Spagnoli was long synonymous with poverty but collective efforts from residents have transformed the neighbourhood into an important heritage site that proudly welcomes visitors. Yet life is still challenging and incomes are meagre. People adapt in creative ways that might look interesting and even charming to us. But these are real people living real lives in a real place. Their hardship isn't fodder for our film rolls. Our presence in small places like this is a privilege, akin to being invited into someone's home. The difference between engaging and gawking is the first step towards travelling better.

LISTINGS

Best Places for...

€ Budget €€ Midrange €€€ Top End

Eating

Classic Neapolitan Dishes

O' Vascio €€
 D6
This is the folklore vibe you've been looking for, and the food will not disappoint either. *8pm-midnight Thu-Sat*

Trattoria A Pignata €€
9 D5
Mouthwatering seafood brought in fresh every day and fried to perfection. *noon-3.30pm & 7-11.30pm Tue-Sun*

Ristorante Mattozzi €€
10 D5
More than a century in Piazza di Carità makes this place a *garanzia* (winner). Sleeper candidate for best pizza in town. *11am-midnight*

Le Zendraglie €€
11 D4
Don't fear the *trippa* (tripe), embrace it! *9am-8pm Mon-Sat*

Salumeria Malinconico €€
12 B2
It's been perfecting its paninis and homemade parmigiana for more than a century, and it shows. *8.30am-2.30pm & 4.30-8pm Mon-Sat*

'O Sfizio €€
 E5
Speaking of parmigiana, almost no one does it better than this tiny yet mighty hometown joint. *7am-7pm Mon-Sat*

Hosteria Toledo €€
 D6
Family-run since the 1950s and serving comforting classics such *risotto alla pescatore* (fish risotto), accompanied by excellent locally sourced wines. *noon-4pm & 7pm-1am Wed-Mon*

Singing for Your Dinner

Casa d' 'e Femminielli €€
 D6
The singing and dancing would be kitsch anywhere else but the *spaghetti alla Nerano* more than makes up for it. *12.30-3pm & 7.30-11pm Tue-Sun*

Trattoria da Nennella €€
 D4
The TikTok gang have descended but it's still a fine place for a good *ragù* and better drama. *12-3pm & 6-11 pm Mon-Sat*

Toledo Street Food

La Passione di Sofi €
17 D7
Nothing beats a freshly fried *cuoppo* (seafood served in a cone) from this neighbourhood institution, where the fish is as fresh as the conversation amongst the locals waiting in line. *10.30am-10pm Mon-Fri, to midnight Sat & Sun*

Spuzzuliann pe' Tuledo €
18 D4
Calzone, *arancini* (deep-fried rice balls) and *crocché di patate* (potato croquettes) all pass muster at this Via Toledo spot that knows its way around a fryer. *10am-10.30pm Sun-Thu, from 10.30am Fri & Sat*

Quartieri Spagnoli Street Food

O' cuop sapurit friggitoria €
19 C6

As far as street food goes, you're in the best place on the best street, so you can't go wrong. 10am-6pm

Con Mollica o Senza €
20 D4

One of the greatest sandwich shops in Naples, if not the world. 8.30am-9pm

Unparalleled Pizza

Sorbillo Pizza a Portafoglio €
21 D7

The lines are worth it for the scalding hot, fresh margarita that you'll cradle in your hands like a pro. 11am-10pm Sun-Thu, to 11pm Fri & Sat

Antica Pizza Fritta da Zia Esterina Sorbillo €
22 D7

Massive pizza fritta, deep-fried pizza dough traditionally filled with dried lard, *provola*, ricotta and tomato. 11am-10pm Mon-Thu, to 11pm Fri & Sun, to midnight Sat

Pizzeria da Attilio €€
23 D4

Must-try pizzas include the sun-shaped Carnevale, the eight points of its crust filled with ricotta. noon-4pm & 7pm-midnight Mon-Sat

Antica Pizzeria e Trattoria al '22 €€
24 D4

As famous for its parmigiana as it is for its pizza, this family spot is lively for lunch or dinner. 11am-4pm & 6.30-11.30pm Mon-Thu, to 11.45pm Fri & Sat

Something for a Sweet Tooth

Pintauro €
25 D7

Said to be founded by the man who stole the *sfogliatella* (sweetened ricotta pastry) recipe from the Sisters of Santa Rosa, this pastry shop deserves our thanks. 9.30am-8pm Wed-Mon

Sfogliatella Mary €
26 D7

At the Via Toledo entrance to Galleria Umberto I, this tiny takeaway vendor is widely considered the queen of the *sfogliatella*. 8am-8.30pm Tue-Sun

Il Gelato Mennella €
see **22** D7

Quality ingredients, handmade cones, and a strict number system mean the best gelato in town, delivered to you on time. 10am-11.30pm Mon-Fri, to 1am Sat & Sun

Drinking

Coffee Day and Night

Caffè Gambrinus
27 D8

The Naples mainstay is an obligatory stop for anyone passing through the city. 7am-1am Sun-Fri, to 2am Sat

Il Vero Bar del Professore
28 D8

It's become a tourist fixture but nothing beats its signature Caffe del Nonno (coffee with hazelnut cream) first thing in the morning. 6am-midnight Sun-Fri 6am-1.30am Sat

Don Café Street Art Coffee
29 C5

One of the last surviving *cuccumella* (flip coffee maker) baristas in town, and also one of the nicest. 9am-9pm Wed-Mon, to 1.30am Fri & Sat

Aperitivo in Quartieri Spagnoli

Ex Falegnameria
30 D6

You'll feel like you've stumbled into someone's living room because, well, you have. Lucky you. *4.30pm-midnight*

Cammarota Spritz
🔵 **31** C5

Join a mix of languages and lifestyles all united in the name of a One Euro Spritz. *noon-midnight Tue & Thu-Sat, from 4pm Mon & Wed*

La Bodega de D10S
see 🟠 **19** C6

Without Don Antonio there would hardly be a Quartieri Spagnoli; go for a drink and ask him why. *9am-7.30pm*

A'picio Spritz
🔵 **32** C6

A friendly, cash-only spot to base yourself and make friends with neighbourhood lads who'll adopt you. *hours vary*

Cocktails and Wine in Toledo

Anthill Cocktail Bar & Tapas
🔵 **33** D6

A swanky rooftop bar where reservations are a must and every drink is an experience. *6pm-2am Tue-Sun*

Astronomia Bar Segreto
🔵 **34** D5

A speakeasy that'll take a moment to find but is well worth the search for inspired drinks and service. *8pm-2am Tue-Sun*

Spuzzulè Winebar
🔵 **35** D7

Fabulous selection of local wines as well as biodynamic labels plus a perfect menu of dishes to pair. *5pm-midnight Tue-Sun*

Malocchio
🔵 **36** D3

Just a few steps from Piazza Dante with great drinks, generous snacks, and a healthy dose of tarot card magic. *6pm-2am, to 3am Fri & Sat*

Shopping

Old School Shops

Talarico
🟣 **37** D5

The late great Mario Talarico and his nephew have turned the humble umbrella into a work of art. *8am-8pm Mon-Sat*

Gino Ramaglia
🟣 **38** D1

This historic art supplies store has been in business since 1926 and counts Andy Warhol among the client list. *8.30am-2pm & 4-7.30pm Mon-Sat*

Via Toledo Boutiques

Mondadori
🟣 **39** D7

Massive new bookstore in the Galleria Umberto I with great spots for reading, working and cafe seating. *10am-8pm*

DieciDieci
🟣 **40** D7

Two-floor boutique with a good mix of Italian labels for women at prices that won't make you go to confession afterwards. *10.30am-8pm*

Gourmet Goodies

Gay Odin
🟣 **41** D3

Famous for its delectable artisanal chocolates, this is the place to indulge. *9.30am-8pm Mon-Sat, 10am-2pm Sun*

La Fabbrica delle Meraviglie
🟣 **42** D7

Tucked behind the Fontana di Nettuno, this wonderland of homegrown sweets and chocolates will be on social media soon enough. *9am-midnight*

See p72 for eating, drinking and shopping listings

Explore
La Sanità & Capodimonte

North of the Centro Storico, La Sanità was once home to noble villas; the fresh air, abundant water and ancient burial grounds were believed to grant the area magical healing powers. Ironically, the 18th-century bridge connecting Piazza del Plebiscito to the Royal Palace at Capodimonte isolated the neighbourhood, and social decline swiftly followed. For centuries, even the dead were afraid to roam in Sanità.

Now, thanks to the dedication of a cluster of cultural associations, Sanità is one of the most vibrant areas in Naples. Everywhere, images of the iconic comedian and neighbourhood native Totò hang proudly. There is laughter once again among the living, and plenty for visitors to see, do and experience.

Getting Around

 Metro

Piazza Cavour station (Line 2) skirts the southern edge of La Sanità, running west to Chiaia (Piazza Amedeo) and Mergellina and east to Napoli Centrale. It's connected to Museo station (Line 1), useful for Vomero (Piazza Vanvitelli) and Municipio.

 Bus

Route C51 runs through La Sanità to Cimitero delle Fontanelle. Routes R2 and 178 run north along Via Toledo to Catacombe di San Gennaro and Capodimonte.

Palazzo Reale di Capodimonte (p67)
GIMAS/SHUTTERSTOCK ©

★
THE BEST

REGAL MUSEUM Museo di Capodimonte (p67)

PANORAMIC VIEWS Palazzo Reale di Capodimonte (p67)

UNDERGROUND GRAVEYARD Catacombe di San Gennaro (p70)

HIDDEN GREEK RUINS Ipogeo dei Cristallini (p70)

REBORN CHURCH La Chiesa di Santa Maria Maddalena ai Cristallini (p71)

★ **TOP EXPERIENCE**

Palazzo Reale di Capodimonte

Originally designed as a hunting lodge for Charles VII of Bourbon, this monumental palace was begun in 1738 and took more than a century to complete. It's now home to southern Italy's largest and richest art gallery. Waiting beyond it is the Parco di Capodimonte, Naples' glorious, green, panoramic lungs.

The Farnese Collection

The **Museo di Capodimonte** famously houses part of the Farnese Collection, inherited by Charles VII of Bourbon from his mother, Elisabetta Farnese. Highlights include Botticelli's *Madonna with Child and Angels,* Bellini's *Transfiguration* and Parmigianino's *Antea.* The Gallery of Rare Objects features such incredible oddities as the bejewelled coffin commissioned in 1548 by Cardinal Alessandro Farnese.

Other Collections

Due to a refit that will make the museum almost entirely energy efficient, collections will close on a rolling basis until December 2025. Consult the website for openings of the Oltre Caravaggio collection, the impressive Neapolitan baroque paintings, and the stunning Porcelain Room in the Royal Apartment.

The Royal Wood

The 134-hectare park is one of the city's green lungs, and a great place for a walk, run, or refuge. Start from the Porta di Mezzo (Middle Gate), where five paths radiate into the woods from the museum. The palace website includes a map of the park, complete with a series of themed walks.

PLANNING TIP
Don't miss the **Tower Garden** in the Royal Wood, home to a wood burning oven where in 1889, pizza with tomato and mozzarella was created, taking the name 'Pizza Margherita', dedicated to Queen Margherita of Savoy.

Scan to purchase tickets online.

Walk the Holy Mile in Sanità

The Holy Mile (the Miglio Sacro) is a sacred, one-mile long itinerary, from the Catacombs of St Gennaro to his relics in the Duomo. But the route also passes through some of the most colourful (and delicious) spots in Sanità, a neighbourhood bursting with colourful street art, bustling cafes and vibrant open-air markets.

START	END	LENGTH
Basilica di San Gennaro Fuori le Mura	Palazzo dello Spagnuolo	2.5km; three hours

1 The Historical Church
Like the catacombs just underneath it, the **Basilica di San Gennaro Fuori le Mura** (beyond the walls) was abandoned in the 5th century. However, the church has recently been brought back to life and now hosts art exhibits for community groups.

2 The Heart of the Hood
Piazza Sanità, with murals of Totò and Maradona, is a vibrant square framed by the Basilica di Santa Maria della Sanità, where a double curved staircase creates a regal yet peaceful ambiance. If you want to go darker, the Catacombe di San Gaudioso is right off the piazza and a fascinating relic of Sanità's history.

3 The Other Veiled Statue
The baroque facade of the **Basilica di San Severo** is juxtaposed with a contemporary mural from urban artists Matu & Sal. Inside, the piece de resistance is the *Figlio Velato,* a 2019 sculpture by Italian artist Jago that complements the iconic *Cristo Velato* in the *centro storico*.

4 Painted Churches and Pastry Arts
The brightly painted **La Chiesa di Santa Maria Maddalena ai Cristallini** celebrates community and features tributes to migrants lost at sea. After feasting on colour, head to Pasticceria Poppella (p73) for a *'fiocco di neve',* a cream-filled bun that is obligatory for all visitors.

5 The Palazzo and the Pizza
The **Palazzo Sanfelice** is a perfect example of the ornate noble residences that once dotted Sanità and there are still plenty of details of its former glory. Don't miss Concettina ai Tre Santi (p72) next door for one of the best pizzas in Naples (no small feat).

6 Mansions and Markets
The **Palazzo dello Spagnuolo** is one of the most well-maintained former noble residences in Naples. If you're looking for a slice of life in Sanità wander through the Mercato dei Vergini (p73), a market teeming with fruits, vegetables and homewares that stretches to Porta San Gennaro.

EXPERIENCES

Examine the Catacombs of San Gennaro
ARCHAEOLOGICAL SITE

MAP: **1** P66 **B2**

After his beheading in Pozzuoli in 305, San Gennaro was most likely taken 'beyond the walls' to this pre-Christian, two-level catacomb carved into tuff stone. His body was later stolen and moved to Benevento in the 9th century, though his head stayed behind in Naples: it wasn't until the 16th century that he was reunited with himself in the *succorpo* (underground vault) of the Duomo. But the centuries where his body lay in these catacombs are amongst the most important for his faithful.

The **Catacombe di San Gennaro** (*catacombedinapoli.it; €9*) makes for a great hour-long, fully accessible visit. The ethereal glow of the catacombs is enhanced by special lighting to protect the frescoes and the entire complex stays at a cool 15°C all year round. You must go on guided visits, but they are offered in Italian and English and are conducted by scholars who are all members of the Paranza Cultural Association. The catacombs were neglected for many years but the Paranza helped to revive them.

Wander a Good Luck Cemetery
CEMETERY

MAP: **2** P66 **A4**

Originally a charnel house in the 1600s, the **Cimitero delle Fontanelle** (*cimiterofontanelle.com; free*) became a mass grave when the plague arrived in 1656 and killed half the population of Naples. It was so full of remains that during one particularly dramatic storm, the city was flooded with skulls and bones. By the 1870s, a cult of devotees developed out of female workers who were tasked with organising the remains. They named the skulls, spoke to them, and brought offerings; this turned the skulls into good luck charms.

Ironically, the cemetery closed during the COVID-19 pandemic and structural works were undertaken to shore up the tuff caves. However, these works seem to conclude and begin again at random, a reminder of just how fragile a place this is. If you want to try to visit, consult the website and call to arrange a guided tour. It is worth trying!

Dig into Greek Ruins
ARCHAEOLOGICAL SITE

MAP: **3** P66 **D5**

Sanità and its surroundings certainly are leaning into a theme. Reopened to the public in 2022 after a mere 2300 years underground, the **Ipogeo dei Cristallini** (*ipogeodeicristallini.org; €10*) is a complex of Hellenistic burial grounds that are accessed via house number 133 on Via dei Cristallini. What do you have in your basement?

Hypogea, meaning underground chambers, were located all over

Neopolis and used for various purposes. But in Sanità, even 2500 years ago, these spaces were devoted to the dead. Carved into the tuff side by side, the four tombs each feature a vestibule where funeral rites would have been delivered, with ornate decor that has been meticulously restored by archaeologists with the support of cultural organisations in Rione Sanità.

It's a quick place to visit and even with a guided tour (€18), you'll be in and out in less than an hour. But afterward, every *palazzo* you pass will make you wonder what lurks beneath. Doubtless, it's something priceless.

Admire a Community Church   CHURCH

MAP: 4 P66 D4

There might be no better place that captures the resilience, creativity and humanity of Sanità than **La Chiesa di Santa Maria Maddalena ai Cristallini** *(10am-1pm; admission free)*. Located on the same block where the Camorra once detonated car bombs, the church had been abandoned for years. But through the efforts of the Paranza collective and a group of young artists, the church was reclaimed and turned into an artistic masterpiece, awash in soothing shades of blue.

The walls are adorned with faces of people in the neighbourhood, and symbolic imagery represents their multifaith culture. Tributes

NO PLACE LIKE HOME
The **Casa Natale di Totò** (MAP: 5 P66 **C4**) is the childhood home of one of Italy's most famous actors, Totò, who grew up in the heart of Sanità. A neighbourhood association hangs handwritten signs indicating which flat was his, and they'll show you the stairwell leading up to Totò's door. It would have been a grim place, and his would have been a grim life. But there are slivers of light that fall onto dusty stairwells and when the wind blows, the cobwebs dance like marionettes in the shadows. Totò's house may one day become a museum, but for now, it's a monument to his melancholy, his mirth and his humble roots. A neighbourhood association takes donations to maintain the small site, and any amount is appreciated.

are tucked like easter eggs, from the unknown skulls buried in the catacombs to portraits of anonymous eyes. But perhaps the most important part of the church is the heart of it. The main altar is crafted from the remains of a migrant boat found off the coast of Lampedusa and transformed by inmates from the infamous Secondigliano Prison in Naples. Call it penance, maybe. Or maybe a bit of grace.

LISTINGS

Best Places for...

€ Budget **€€** Midrange **€€€** Top End

See p66 for map of locations

Eating

Miraculous Pizza

Lombardi 1892 €€
6 D6

It's been around for over a century, but that doesn't mean it's lost any of its charm, or flavour. *12.15-3.15pm & 7.15-11.30pm Tue-Sun*

Pizzeria Starita €€
7 B5

A constant contender for best in the city, and even if it's franchised, it's still stellar. *noon-3.30pm & 7pm-midnight Tue-Sun*

Pizzeria Oliva di Carla e Salvatore €€
8 B4

This is where other chefs go when they're looking for a good pizza. *11.30am-4pm & 6.30-11.30pm*

Concettina ai Tre Santi €€
9 C5

It may be part of the glitterati on Capri in summer, but come here year-round for the real deal. *noon-midnight Mon-Sat, to 5pm Sun*

Isabella de Cham Pizza Fritta €€
10 C5

Rising star Isabella de Cham is at the helm of this all-female-run pizzeria specialising in fried pizza with a twist. *11am-4pm & 7-11pm Mon-Sat, 11-4pm Sun*

La Taverna di Totò €€
11 C4

Bustling local spot for faithfully executed pizzas and a good selection of antipasti and fried treats. *12-3.30pm & 7-11pm Tue-Sun*

Pizzeria Miracoli F.lli Esposito €€
12 D5

In a land of world-renowned pizzas, this is the spot that might just be your favourite. Go for the marinara and tell your friends you were there in the beginning. *8.30am-11.30pm Wed-Mon*

Home Cooking

La Locanda del Monacone €€
13 C4

Order *linguine alla Luciana* and a litre of red wine with peaches, like Totò would have wanted. *12-3.30pm & 7-10.30pm Thu-Tue*

Cantina del Gallo €€
14 A5

Get spoiled by a nonna on *calzoncini* (stuffed wood-fired pizza dough) or the signature *A'Cafona*, a delightfully garlicky affair. *11am-4pm & 7pm-midnight*

Pizzeria Trattoria La Taverna del Re a Capodimonte €€
15 C2

Opposite the Museo di Capodimonte, this neighbourly trattoria offers a short menu of uncomplicated, classic dishes that hit the spot after a day in the park. *noon-3.30pm & 7-11pm Tue-Sun*

Trattoria Addù Rosettin €€
16 C5

Welcoming, unpretentious neighbourhood

spot serving classics like *gnocchi alla Sorrentina* and lemon tarts. *12-4pm & 6-11pm*

Tasty Pastries

Pasticceria Poppella €
17 D5
If you've come to Naples and haven't had a *fiocco di neve* from Poppella, you technically aren't allowed to leave. *6am-10pm*

Pasticceria Di Costanzo €
18 D6
Technicolour and technique combine to form sweet treats that Instagram dreams are made of. *7.15am-8.15pm Thu-Tue*

Cioccolato Mario Gallucci €
19 C4
Hidden away down a Sanità side street, this vintage chocolatier has been ruining waistlines since 1890. *8.30am-1pm & 2-7pm Mon-Fri, to 1pm Sat*

Pasticceria Mignone €
20 D6
Beautiful homemade cakes as well as excellent renditions of classic Neapolitan pastries that will satisfy any sweet tooth. *7.15am-8pm Tue-Sun*

Drinking

Coffee Stops in Sanità

Caffè del Principe
21 B4
A humble bar in the thick of it all, named for Totò (he was nicknamed 'Il Principe') and serving very decent espresso. *7am-9pm Mon-Fri, to 11pm Sat, 7am-2pm & 5-11pm Sun*

Caffetteria Santoro
22 C4
Dependably good coffee with servers who know everyone's name and treat them like old friends. *6.30am-8.30pm Mon-Sat, to 2pm Sun*

Wine, Beer and Cocktails

Antica Cantina Sepe
23 D5
This unlikely hotspot has on-tap local vino for €1.50 a glass and lots of other bottles that won't break the bank. Grab some groceries while you're here as well. *9am-8.30pm, to midnight Thu*

El Pocho Pub
see **8** B4
Imagine getting the best burger of your life in the middle of Naples, whilst looking at giant murals of Italian film stars? Add €3 Peronis to the mix and you've got a deal. *12-4pm & 6.30pm-4am Tue-Sun*

Shopping

Handmade Treasures

Omega
24 C6
Handmade leather gloves are meticulously crafted using a traditional 25-step process. Best of all, they retail for a fraction of the price charged by luxury fashion houses. *8.30am-6pm Mon-Fri*

Vincenzo Oste Gioielli
25 D5
Extraordinary, sinuous design pieces in sterling silver that look and feel like wearable art from the son of artist Annibale Oste. Check out the luxe art hotel he and wife Ines created. *9am-5pm Mon-Fri*

Mercato dei Vergini
26 D5
One of the city's most historic market streets. There are still plenty of shoemakers, seamstresses and confectioners to be found among the fruit and vegetable stands. *7am-1pm*

★ WORTH A TRIP

Certosa e Museo di San Martino

What was once a panoramic home for Carthusian monks is now a museum of 'memories' of Neapolitan history. From dazzling baroque interiors to one of the country's finest cloisters, its eclectic array of treasures includes precious paintings, royal barges, and an important collection of *presepi napoletani* (Neapolitan nativity cribs). And of course, don't forget the view: it too is one of the great treasures of Naples.

PLANNING TIP
Head back down to the Quartieri Spagnoli via the Pedamentina di San Martino stairs tucked behind the stone wall directly facing the shops or cross over to the iconic **Salita del Petraio** for the view that has inspired artists for centuries.

Get tickets via the Musei Italiani app.

Chiesa della Certosa

Both the facade and the spectacular inlaid marble interior of the **church** were designed by Cosimo Fanzago between 1623 and 1656, making it among the most splendid baroque examples in the city. Orazio De Orio added the wooden choir, while the marble statues representing Courage and Charity are by Giuseppe Sanmartino, sculptor of the *Cristo Velato* in Naples' Cappella Sansevero (p40). The stunning sacristy contains ceiling frescoes by Cavalier d'Arpino, while the Cappella del Tesoro houses Jusepe de Ribera's Pietà and Luca Giordano's vault masterpiece *Triumph of Judith*.

Chiostro Grande

Designed by Giovanni Antonio Dosio in the late 16th century and revamped by Cosimo Fanzago in the 17th century, the **Chiostro Grande** (pictured) is widely considered one of the finest cloisters in Italy. Refined Tuscan-Doric porticoes frame the courtyard, itself dotted with vibrant camellias. The balustrade – capped by skulls designed by Fanzago – marks the area once used as the monastery's cemetery.

ENRICO DELLA PIETRA/SHUTTERSTOCK ©

Treasures of the Galleries

The *Immagini e Memorie di Napoli della Città e del Regno di Napoli* (Images and Memories of the City and Kingdom of Naples) is home to the *Tavola Strozzi*, a detailed oil-on-wood depiction of 15th-century Naples. The Sezione Navale houses a small but important collection of royal barges, while the Sezione Presepiale is famous for its colossal Presepe Cuciniello, arguably the most important of all the city's *presepi* (nativity cribs). The Quarto del Priore is home to Pietro Bernini's sculpture *Madonna and Child with the Infant John the Baptist.* Don't miss the sweeping view from the Loggia del Priore in the Quarto del Priore gallery, taking in the Prior's private garden, the eastern side of Naples and Mt Vesuvius.

QUICK BREAK
For craft beers and artisanal coffees, head over to nearby **Ventimetriquadri** *(facebook.com/ ventimetriquadri. specialtycoffee)* in Vomero.

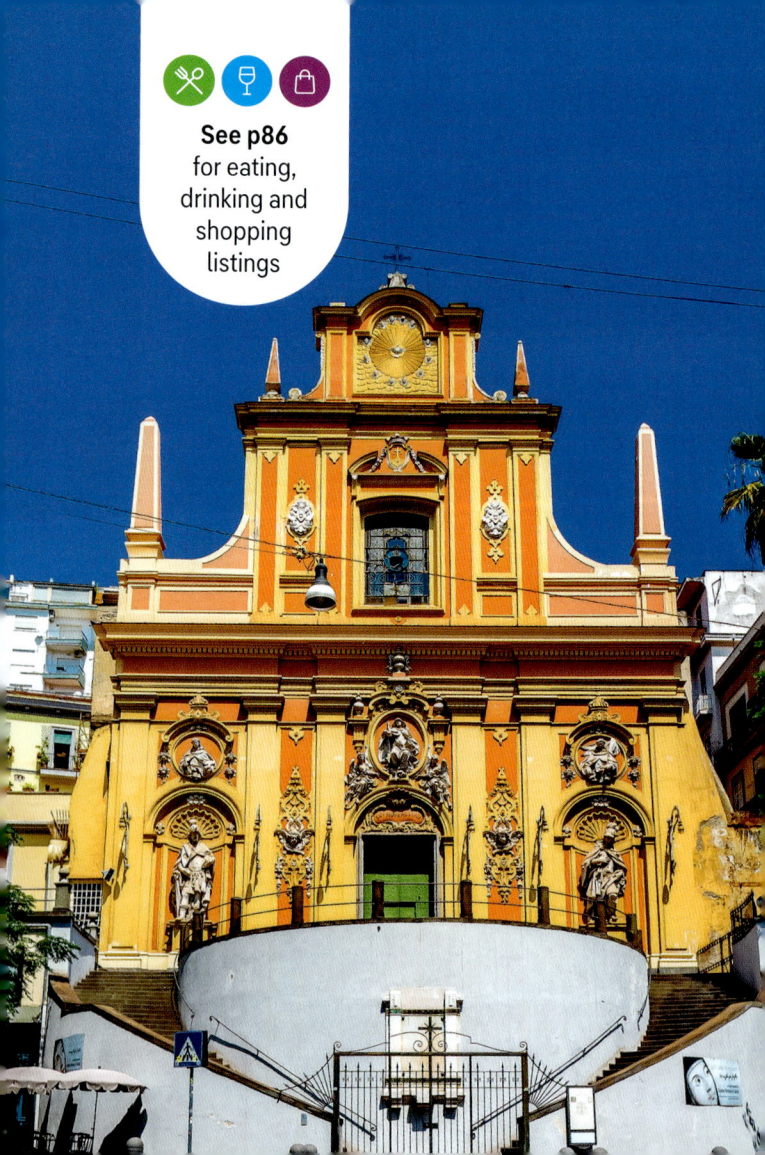

See p86 for eating, drinking and shopping listings

Explore
Santa Lucia & Chiaia

Naples is a dance between land and sea. From the hills, the Mediterranean is a distant mirror, glimmering toward the horizon. The densely populated centre drowns out the crashing waves but there is an echo of a faraway waltz. Then the first slivers of azure appear beyond Piazza del Plebescito and songs of Santa Lucia waft through the air.

Perched above the seafront, leafy Chiaia boasts boutique hotels in preserved palaces. The world comes to be measured and fitted by the neighbourhood's famous tailors, who set up shop at dawn, arranging their pristine wares by the light of the rising sun. And where else would one go to look their best? The great mirror of the sea beckons, reflecting the very best of us.

Getting Around

 Metro

There is a lot of infrastructure development in and around the port which means great connections between Napoli Centrale on lines 1 (Università) and 2 (Amadeo). More work is scheduled which will cut travel time even further. The long awaited line 6 is finally open, connecting Chiaia with Municipo station in the centre.

 Walk

Walking along the *lungomare* (waterfront) is a well-established pastime in these parts, so if you're not in a rush, it's the way to go. Chiaia is connected via not insubstantial staircases but they're wide and accommodating.

THE BEST

TAILOR-MADE EXPERIENCE
E Marinella (p84)

EGG-CELLENT ADVENTURE
Castel dell'Ovo (p85)

ROYAL TUNNELLING Galleria Borbonica (p85)

FISHING VILLAGE Borgo Marinaro (p84)

FANTASY FOOTBALL Stadio Diego Armando Maradona (p84)

Chiesa di Santa Teresa a Chiaia (p81)
NEKOMURA/SHUTTERSTOCK ©

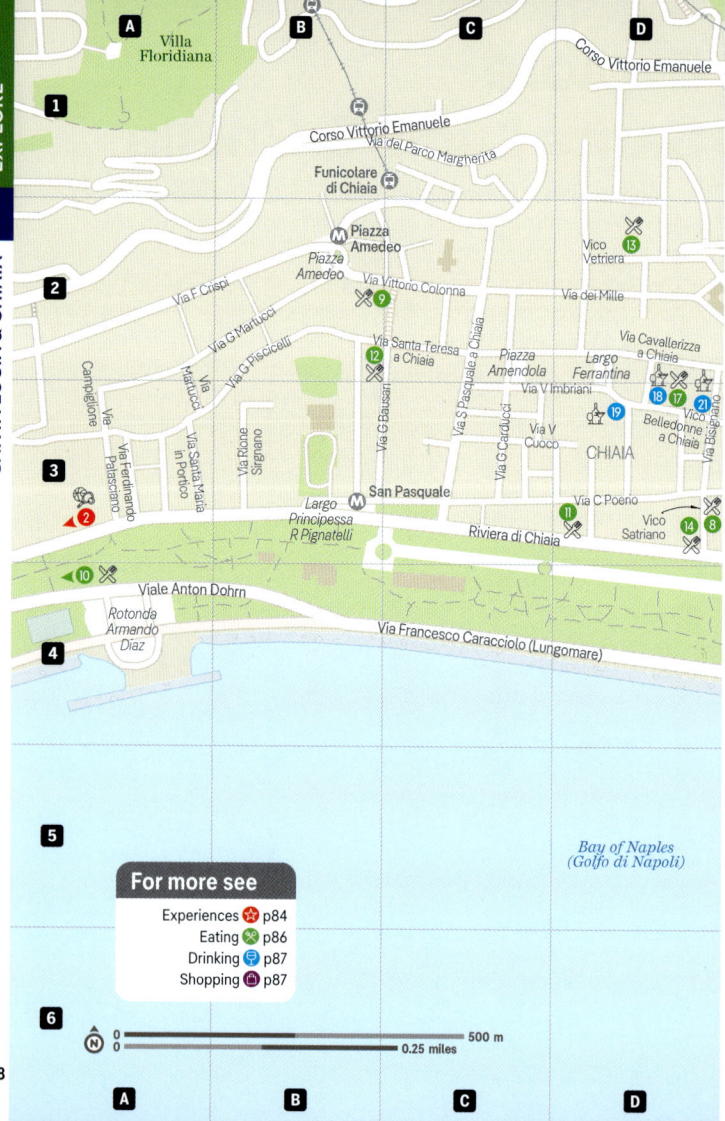

WALKING TOUR

Walk Classical Chiaia

For centuries, Chiaia was the patrician centre of Naples: refined, stately and made for strolling. Though times have changed and the neighbourhood is much buzzier with trendy restaurants and shops, the old-school charm still remains. This is the bucolic heart of the city, with promenades on the sea and homes that housed local dynasties.

START	END	LENGTH
Villa Maria	Castel dell'Ovo	2.2km; 1½ hours

1 Artsy Architecture

Just off the northern end of Piazza Amedeo, colourful **Villa Maria** is an outstanding example of Italian art nouveau architecture. Dating from 1901, the building was commissioned by French entrepreneur Giulio Huraut and designed by Veneto architect Angelo Trevisan as the Grand Eden Hotel, a luxury slumber pad for wealthy foreign travellers.

2 Baroque Jewels

From the piazza, it's a *flaneur's* stroll into Passeggiata Colonna, an outdoor arcade flanked by small boutiques. Turn left into Via Vittorio Colonna (which becomes Via dei Mille) and you'll pass the dazzling baroque **Chiesa di Santa Teresa a Chiaia**, designed by Cosimo Fanzago and home to paintings by Luca Giordano.

3 Optical Illusions

Via dei Mille eventually kinks southeast, becoming Via Filangieri, home to art nouveau **Palazzo Mannajuolo**. Wander inside to admire the optical illusion of its spiral staircase. The staircase is inside a private residence, so be prepared to be met by a custodian who might not care about your Instagram feed.

4 The Piazza Kings

At the end of Via Filangieri, turn right into Via Santa Caterina. The street spills into **Piazza dei Martiri**, its 19th-century centrepiece dedicated to Neapolitan martyrs. Palazzo Calabritto (No 30) was designed by architect Luigi Vanvitelli, famous for his monumental Reggia di Caserta.

5 Memorable Villas

When exigent Sir Ferdinand Acton, a minister at the court of King Ferdinand IV (1759–1825), asked Pietro Valente to design his residence in 1826, Valente whipped up this monument to neo-classical architecture. Now it's the **Museo Pignatelli**, whose aristocratic collection is an exquisite time capsule, topped off by the 19th- and 20th-century carriages in the adjoining Museo delle Carrozze.

6 Picturesque Playgrounds

Head south on Via Calabritto and turn right into Riviera di Chiaia, onto the former Bourbon garden now known as the **Villa Comunale**. Dividing the Riviera di Chiaia from Via Caracciolo and the sea, this is the neighbourhood's communal backyard, complete with roller-skating rink and bandstand.

7 Eggstrordinary Monuments

Turn left onto Via Partenope (Lungomare), a pedestrianised seafront promenade popular with everyone from love-struck couples to Neapolitan families. The strip leads to Via Eldorado and the ancient islet of Borgo Marinaro, home to the **Castel dell'Ovo** (p85) and its silver-screen–worthy rooftop views.

WALKING TOUR
Walk a Sartorial Street Tour

Chiaia is home to excellent independent shops ranging from vintage to high fashion. But for a true experience, stop into the storied tailors that make this neighbourhood world famous. They'll spoil you with a coffee, a conversation, and clothes as sharp as cut glass. If you've ever wanted the bespoke experience now's the time, and the place.

START	END	LENGTH
E Marinella	L'Antiquario	4km; 1½ hours

1 The Silk Tie Masters

Start your shopping hunt with the centrepiece of any classic look, and consult the masters of the silk tie at **E Marinella** (p84). It's been in this tiny Chiaia storefront for generations and owner Maurizio Marinella is there all day every day, keeping it elegant with ties, scarves and a line of cashmere.

2 Bespoke Indulgence

It's only been eight generations of sartorial rigour but **Cilento** and his team seem to have got it right, from shoes to sweaters. Step into this regal fitting room and prepare to be pampered by tailors who've been trained to find your good side with a combination of sartorial magic and Neapolitan hospitality.

3 Luxe Links

Imagine going to all the trouble of getting a suit made and not getting the right cufflinks. Such things are simply not done, and certainly not when you've got **Barbarulo Napoli** at the ready. With handmade collections for women and men, this is that *tocca finale* (finishing touch) that you can't miss. Check out its Mediterranean collection for swirling colour palettes that will pop on your wrist.

4 Historic Houses

From crisp shirts and blazers to safari looks and plush polos, the historic house of **Mariano Rubinacci** creates lifetime looks to measure. There's also a full range of accessories and a luxe line for pets, including collars, bandanas and blankets. It'll all cost you a pretty penny but it's not every day you get to dress yourself in history.

5 The Artful Shirtmaker

You could order your shirt online but then you'd miss the joy of touching the paper silhouette of your shirt that **Camiceria Piccolo** stores in their archives. Shirtmaking has been elevated to an art form here, and you'll walk away with an entirely new appreciation for it.

6 Dashing Drams

What better way to celebrate sartorial victory than in one of the best bars in the world? You'll need to book a table in **L'Antiquario** (p87), but you'll be at home in this tiny Chiaia speakeasy amongst the nattily dressed Naples set. All the better to swap stories and style tips over the best French 75 you've ever had.

EXPERIENCES

Pick Your Perfect Tie

SHOPPING

MAP: ❶ P78 E3

For more than a century, **E Marinella** *(emarinella.eu)* has dressed kings and presidents in silks and particularly ties, its iconic signature patterns forming an unspoken bond between their wearers. Every day, owner Maurizio Marinella skilfully advises clients whilst offering his special coffee. Come Christmastime, he'll be on Via Rivieria di Chiaia handing out hot chocolate with a spirit that rivals the nativity scenes down the road.

But the Marinella generosity doesn't end there. For no charge, you can visit the tiny workshop down the road. Meet the team of tailors who work methodically to perfect every stitch, get a lesson in the archival patterns that each tell a story, and order your own bespoke tie. And of course, Maurizio will invite you for a coffee. The visit takes about an hour but the memory will stick with you for a lot longer. This is Naples at its best.

Head to the Match of the Day

FOOTBALL MATCH

MAP: ❷ P78 A3

In Naples, few places are more sacred than **Stadio Diego Armando Maradona** *(sscnapoli.it/en/)*. Watching the resident SSC Napoli football (soccer) team is more than a sport here, it is a form of devotion. If you do one holy thing, make it to a match. Like many stadiums, the stands are divided here to keep opposing teams apart. You're best choosing the Distinti section, and prices will vary according to how low you go. The two end sections known as the Curva (A and B) are home to the Ultras, the fervent fans who are unabashedly passionate about their team. It's probably better to witness their support from your distinti seats than it is to join them.

The acoustics are shattering: the noise of the crowd is almost primal, a roar that will echo whether the team is doing well or not. Get into it and don't be afraid to ask someone next to you for explanations if you need them. This is Naples at its finest, and you'll never feel closer to the city.

Meet Cutes in Borgo Marinaro

PORT

The **Borgo Marinaro** (MAP: ❸ P78 G6) is the sort of place you'd want to set up a meet cute because it's got all the elements of a rom-com: bobbing boats sitting idly by seaside cafes and restaurants framed by happy-looking plants and happier-looking couples. Head down here almost any day of the year and you'll have some of the best people-watching opportunities in Italy.

Grab a seat at the very old school **Club Nautico della Vela** (MAP: ❹ P78 G6) and close your eyes: listen to the sounds of children jumping into the sea and the parents pretending to scold them before they join in. The limpid water will gently lap at the wooden docks, and you'll swear that you've dreamt this exact scene. And maybe you have. Maybe this will be the place that you remember forever.

Tunnel Down into the Galleria Borbonica
HISTORIC SITE

MAP: 5 P78 F3

Royals, they're just like us! Except for how they get their very own tunnels dug between their palaces and military barracks in the event that the rest of us get wise and decide to revolt. The **Galleria Borbonica** *(galleriaborbonica.com)* was commissioned by Ferdinand II in 1853 for this very purpose and was dug into the 17th-century Bolla Aqueduct system, because who needs water when you've got an escape from people you exploit?

It fell out of use after unification but then became a refuge for nearly 10,000 people during WWII. Take a guided tour through what effectively became a refugee colony complete with playgrounds, communal latrines, and a hospital ward. In the postwar years, the tunnels served as a police impound and there are still classic cars on display. Plus, excavations uncovered fossils, which may well be mermaids. Okay maybe not, but one never really knows.

The very useful website has information on tours, entrances and hours. Keep in mind that there are two entrances (as befits a royal tunnel).

STROLL THE PROMENADE
Okay, here's the thing. The **Lungomare** (MAP: 7 P78 E4) on Via Partenope is very likely to be crowded with people strolling along the seaside or sitting in overpriced restaurants, well, people-watching. You're not likely to find that hole-in-the-wall place where you'll have a meal of a lifetime and unless you're there very early in the morning, you won't have the place to yourself. But that's the whole point.

Crack into an Egg-cellent Castle
HISTORIC SITE

MAP: 6 P78 G6

This imposing 12th-century Norman **Castel dell'Ovo** sitting on the islet of Megaride is the oldest of seven in the city and has been a monastery, a fortress, a prison and a royal residence. It gets its name (Castle of the Egg) from that absolute joker Virgil who buried an egg where the castle stands today and claimed that when the egg broke, the castle would fall. The legend took on such force that when a footbridge collapsed during Queen Anne's reign she had to announce to the city that the egg had been unharmed.

As of writing the castle is closed, but you can still admire the imposing figure it strikes on the very edge of the Neapolitan coastline. And don't worry, the egg is fine.

LISTINGS

Best Places for...

€ Budget   €€ Midrange   €€€ Top End

> See p78 for map of locations

Eating

Classic Dishes

Signora Bettola €€
8 D3
What if you were transported to a medieval tavern where nativity scenes towered over you while you dined? Find out here. *12.30-4pm & 7.30pm-midnight*

Ristorante Vineria Cap'alice €€
9 B2
A quintessential neighbourhood spot at the bottom of one of Chiaia's signature staircases, you'll never want to leave. *11am-3.30pm & 7.30-11.30pm Mon-Fri, 6.30-11.30pm Sat*

Cibi Cotti €€
10 A4
A true local lunchtime favourite with gems like *pasta e fagioli* (bean and pasta soup) and slow-cooked *ragù*. It buzzes at lunchtime so look out for a table and join the scrum. *noon-3pm*

Romantic Pairings

CrudoRe €€€
11 D3
A heavenly marriage of seafood and wine that will wow anyone from the novice to the sommelier in the family. Worth a detour. *hours vary*

Trattoria dell'Oca €€€
12 B2
Great for a family gathering, a meetup with friends, or a romantic dinner for two. Talk about multitasking. *7.30-11pm Mon-Fri, 12.15-3pm & 7.30-11pm Sat & Sun*

L'Ebbrezza di Noè €€€
13 D2
A wine shop by day, 'Noah's Drunkenness' transforms into an intimate dining experience by night. Try the *paccheri fritti* (fried pasta stuffed with eggplant). *6-11pm Tue-Thu, to midnight Fri & Sat, 1-3pm Sun*

Dialetti €€€
14 D3
What's more intoxicating than a natural wine bar serving beautiful dishes bursting with local ingredients in a sumptuously vintage setting? *6pm-midnight Mon-Fri, noon-3.30pm & 6pm-midnight Sat-Sun*

Seaside Feasts

Club Nautico della Vela €€€
see **4** G6
For old-school vibes reminiscent of yacht club scions and fantastic fish. *hours vary*

Officina del Mare €€€
15 G5
Friendly staff and tons of options for that one dinner you'll think about all the time. *noon-midnight Mon-Fri, 12.30pm-midnight Sat & Sun*

'O Tabaccaro €€€
16 G5
Bustling, noisy, and delightful local spot with a range of options that

will satisfy everyone at the table. *12-2.30pm & 7.30-11.30pm Fri-Wed*

Pescheria Mattiucci €€€
 D3

Every day, this family-run Chiaia fishmonger transforms into a wonderfully intimate, sociable seafood eatery. *12.30-3pm & 7-10.30pm Tue-Sat*

Drinking

Easy Aperitivi

Enoteca Belledonne
 D3

Stellar wine bar with great selections for finger food and a cosy setting that'll take you from day to night in style. *hours vary*

Barril
 D3

What do you do if the bar has more charm than all of you put together? Drink to it, and enjoy the best of Boho chic Naples. *7pm-2am Tue-Thu & Sun, to 3am Fri & Sat*

Cantine Sociali
 E2

It's loud, and crowded, and you might wait, but it's great fun and even better value at this neighbourhood mainstay with great burgers. *6pm-2am Mon-Wed, to 3am Thu-Sat, 7pm-1.40am Sun*

Chic Cocktails

Chandelier
 D3

You'd best reserve a table here but be rewarded with incredible drinks and abundant snacks at this effortlessly cool Chiaia haunt. *5.30pm-2pm*

L'Antiquario
 E4

The only way to get in here is with a reservation but you'll be rewarded with a table at one of the world's best watering holes. *6pm-3am*

Shopping

Chiaia Chic

Chiaja Vintage
23 F2

This beautifully curated collection of vintage bags feels like a museum of wearable art where you can buy a piece of history. *10am-8.30pm Mon-Sat*

Pama Vintage
24 G2

Tucked away in one of the arcades along Via Chiaia, this shop feels like going into the closet of the person whose style you've always envied. *10am-8pm Mon-Sat*

Happy Vintage
25 F2

A little corner of happiness on the Via Chiaia with friendly staff, hard-to-find pieces, and buckets of character. *9.30am-8pm Mon-Sat*

WALKING TOUR

Walk Mergellina

Naples is a city on the sea, defined by the Mediterranean. The seaside Mergellina, a humble corner where fisherman plied their trade in between noble Posillipo and fashionable Chiaia, is the best place to appreciate it. Come for the *graffa* (sweet fried doughnuts), and stay for panoramic views of perfect sunsets over the place they call Partenope.

START	END	LENGTH
Mappatella Beach	Chalet Ciro	4km; 2½ hours

1 Hit the Beach

One of the pure joys of being in Naples is that you're only a short walk from a wonderful beach that's beloved by locals and totally free of charge. You'll never confuse **Mappatella Beach** for the Amalfi Coast, but it's a perfect escape from the heat of the city.

2 Legendary Nonnas

Nonna Anna may be stirring the great saucepot in the sky, but her loud lunch spot kicks on. Hidden in a market arcade, **Cibi Cotti** serves real-deal Neapolitan home-cooking. Order at the counter, wait for a table and enjoy the ruckus.

3 Fishing Villages

La Torretta di Mergellina is a tiny warren of streets where local fishermen once lived and a lovely perch for a post-*pranzo* (post-meal) walk. From Via Piedigrotta, enter the quarter from Via Santa Maria della Neve (which becomes Cupa Caiafa), a skinny street flanked by religious shrines, hung washing and curious locals. Turn left into Via Generale Cucca Camillo to return to Via Piedigrotta.

4 Historic Parks

Head towards Mergellina station and you'll see what looks like a pretty uninviting car tunnel (it is), but you'll also find a path leading up to the **Parco Vergiliano in Piedigrotta**, the supposed burial site of the great poet Virgil and home to the largest Roman tunnel in the world. Although the tunnel might not always be open, even looking through the entrance of it is enough to give you shivers.

5 Postcard Views

The slight trek on the famous Salita della Grotta is well worth it to reach the **Belvedere di Sant'Antonio a Posillipo**, one of the finest viewpoints over the Bay of Naples. On a clear day, you'll see Sorrento in the south, Ischia in front of you, and the Campi Flegrei in the west. If you get there for sunset, prepare to have your breath taken away (even more than you did during the climb up).

6 A Lion's Tale

The battered-looking lion in **Piazzetta del Leone** once stood by a long-gone local date tree *(dattero)*, so famous that it named nearby Vico Dattero. The street itself was known as the Neapolitan Montmartre, a popular haunt for the city's 19th-century painters.

7 A Sweet Finish

Locals triple-park outside **Chalet Ciro**, a retro seafront chalet famous for its *cono graffa,* gelato in a doughnut cone that Neapolitans call a *bomba* (bomb). Or go salty and grab some *taralli caldi* (warm, pretzel-like biscuits) and stroll down the Molo Luise, with a cold beer and the sea in front of you.

★ WORTH A TRIP

Pompeii

The ruins of Pompeii are a veritable time machine, hurling visitors back to the age of emperors and Latin chatter. Here, time remains paused at 79 CE, the city's frescoed homes, businesses and baths still waiting for their occupants to return. Few archaeological sites offer such an intimate connection to the past, and few are as deeply haunting and evocative.

PLANNING TIP
Always plan to enter the park near the Anfiteatro – there are far fewer groups (and thus, crowds) and even on a hot day you'll have plenty of tree-lined real estate. It really does change the experience!

The Amphitheatre

The Romans were nothing if not entertainers, and the 20,000-seat **Anfiteatro** (amphitheatre) on the eastern end of the park is proof of their love for the stage. It's one of the oldest known Roman theatres and hosted nobility, politicians and spectators from neighbouring towns, all of whom came to marvel at the battles. But it's all fun and games until a riot breaks out, and after the ruckus of 59 CE the theatre was shuttered until 62, when a deadly earthquake struck. Frescoes of gladiatorial battles are visible on the parapet and it's one of the best places in Pompeii to get a little retreat from the heat on sunny days. Plus, the theatre is still in use for performances: the OG Gladiator Russell Crowe even returned for a concert.

Pompeii was a pretty wild place in its day, and nowhere tells this better than the amphitheatre. In 59 CE cheers from the crowds led to widespread fisticuffs between spectators from Pompeii and nearby Nocera. As a result of these riots, the Senate of Rome actually closed the arena in Pompeii for 10 years! But the edict was withdrawn after the tragic earthquake in 62 CE, when people wisely decided it was probably time to let off some steam. One of the earliest structures to be unearthed, the amphitheatre was excavated for the first time in 1748.

Scan for practical information.

LARA-SH/SHUTTERSTOCK ©

The Forum

The magnificent rectangular **Foro** (forum) with its limestone columns was Pompeii's main piazza, the seat of religious, commercial and political life. Visit the **Tempio di Giove**, a temple dedicated to Jupiter, Minerva and Juno, and thoughtfully (though in hindsight, ironically) designed to line up with Mt Vesuvius. You'll also find the **Tempio di Apollo**, the **Macellum** (produce market), the **Granai del Foro** (granary), now home to more than 9000 recovered household items, including amphorae and pots, and the magnificent baths. This is the spot that most people identify with Pompeii, and it is certainly the most photographed. However, it isn't the only place to see by far: think of it like the ancient Oxford Circus, Temple Bar, or Times Square. Best to end your day here or at least wait until the sun is not as

QUICK BREAK
Check out **Zi'Caterina** *(noon-midnight)*, a spacious old-school restaurant that looks touristy but serves delicious traditional southern Italian food and is open throughout the day.

high overhead, because even when it isn't summertime, the sun still bakes here.

Il Lupanare

Pompeii's most salacious building, **Il Lupanare** brothel inhabits an area once known as a red-light district. The explicit wall frescoes were an enticement of sorts for clients, who were subsequently 'entertained' in one of the five rooms on the ground floor. Each room featured a stone bed and latrine, and the walls remain etched with the graffiti of its sex workers. That this graffiti is in various languages is telling: most sex workers were enslaved people. The 1st floor harbours another five rooms, assumed to be the sleeping quarters of the workers and the brothel's owner.

Villa dei Misteri

The grand *domus* (homes) in Pompeii, often given nicknames like 'House of the Boar' when the owner is unknown, are revered for their elaborate frescoes and mosaics. A spectacular example is the 90-room seaside **Villa dei Misteri** (Villa of the Mysteries). Its magnificent Dionysiac frieze, a massive fresco covering three walls of the dining room, depicts Dionysus and his wife Ariadne as they welcome a young girl into his cult via ritual flagellation. The fresco is all the more memorable for its startling red background. Miniature Egyptian-inspired paintings can be found in the *tablinum* (study). The villa also includes an area that would have been used to produce wine, and features a rebuilt wooden press. Proving once again that location is always the clincher when it comes to real estate, the complex dates to the 2nd century BCE but would have undergone renovations to its current floor plan around 80 to 70 BCE, when the friezes of the Mysteries would have been added. Although you may have to wait a while to get inside, it is

OPLONTIS AND STABIAE
Oplontis and **Stabiae**, two nearby sites, were also buried in the 79 CE eruption and are part of the Pompeii archaeological park. The villas that have been excavated in each place reveal fascinating glimpses into ancient life and the two sites are almost always blissfully uncrowded. Shuttles bring you to and from the main park, making it an easy way to dive deep.

MORE TIPS

Crowds are always thickest in the morning when large groups come from schools and cruise ships. Take the afternoon to explore.

The excellent audio guides are multilingual and offer various itineraries.

Pompeii is meant to accommodate many people (it's a city, after all). For every crowded spot, there's a quiet block.

You should only buy tickets directly through the Pompei website (not from scalpers).

entirely worth it. Indeed, this is the site within Pompeii that has inspired poets, artists and budding archaeologists for centuries.

Insula dei Casti Amanti

For the first time since the opening of the park, visitors can observe excavations of an ancient block in real time via an elevated path suspended over the **Insula dei Casti Amanti** (House of the Chaste Lovers), the house of the Painters at work and the house of the colonnaded Last Supper. The site was first uncovered in 1912 but recent discoveries include a room decorated with mythological figures, charcoal drawings made by children in a service courtyard, and an entrance hall where two skeletons of victims of the eruption were found. You can watch the process of bringing Pompeii to life as well as an innovative effort to bring photovoltaic panels onto the site on this fully accessible platform, which was designed as part of the 'Pompei for All' initiative. Interestingly, in 2023 two skeletons were discovered in the Insula which were analysed and found to belong to two males whose deaths were likely the result of multiple traumas due to falling debris. However, they were not victims of the pyroclastic flow and pumice that is traditionally thought to be the cause of most destruction in Pompeii. Instead, they are believed to have died in an earthquake that accompanied the eruption and were discovered beneath a wall that had collapsed between the final phase of the deposition of pumice and prior to the arrival of the pyroclastic flows that buried Pompeii for centuries. Finds like this show how much we still have to learn about this place.

Join the Excavations

Every day from Monday to Friday at 11am, groups of up to 15 people can join archaeologists to visit

ANADOLU/GETTY IMAGES ©

active excavation sites in the **Regio IX** neighbourhood (pictured) of the park. The experience allows visitors to observe and engage in ongoing projects, partaking in the painstaking methods that archaeologists and restorers use to bring these fragile places back to life. As it's open air, it's subject to weather and reservations are necessary (though easily made over the phone). This is truly a once-in-a-lifetime experience that budding archaeologists will remember forever. For reservations call +39 327 271 6666 between 9.30am and 1.30pm, Monday to Friday (preferably 48 hours in advance).

TICKETS

Consider buying the three-day card, which gives you access to the main park as well as the sites at Oplontis, Stabiae and Boscoreale and includes a shuttle service.

★ WORTH A TRIP

Mount Vesuvius

The twin-peaked Mt Vesuvius has been erupting for thousands of years – and is still active. While most visitors head straight for its panoramic summit, Vesuvius' fertile slopes are a lesser-known pleasure, laced with walking trails and vineyards that contrast with, and yet strangely complement, the volcano's ominous presence.

PLANNING TIP
The public EAV bus service from Pompeii is cheaper than private shuttles and drops you off at the same point. Ignore touts in Pompeii telling you that the public bus isn't running that day.

Parco Nazionale del Vesuvio

Mt Vesuvius is the focal point of the **Parco Nazionale del Vesuvio** but the national park covers 8482 protected hectares, with rich fauna including around 140 species of birds, hawks and imperial ravens. The volcano's dual summit is also diverse, with classic Mediterranean vegetation on the southern face and a mix of chestnuts, maples and holm oaks on the cooler north-facing slopes of Mt Somma. Nine marked nature trails trace the park, varying in length and difficulty, from the easy 'Vallone della Profica' (1.7km) to the challenging 'Along the Cognoli' (8km). The best route for reaching the crater is the moderately difficult 'Gran Cono' (3.8km). Alternatively, **Horse Riding Tour Naples** runs daily morning and afternoon horse-riding tours of the park, weather permitting. Tours include transfers to/from Naples, Pompeii and Ercolano (Herculaneum).

Gran Cono

Reaching Mt Vesuvius' **Gran Cono** (Great Cone) is a literal and figurative high. The summit crater – 230m deep and 650m in diameter – sits 1282m above sea level, offering a breathtaking panorama that (on a clear day) takes in Naples, the Campi Flegrei and the bay islands. One can also eyeball

Scan for practical information.

VERSA/SHUTTERSTOCK ©

Monte Picentini, part of the Apennines that run down the Italian peninsula. Buses reach the summit car park and ticket office, from where an 860m gravel path leads up to the summit. If arriving by car, the car park is further down the slope but serviced by a shuttle bus (return trip €2). Admission to the summit includes a free guided walk halfway around the crater.

Wine Growing

The first evidence of grape cultivation on Vesuvius dates back to the 5th century BCE. The Vesuvio Lacryma Christi DOC wine is made from native grapes of Mt Vesuvius and pre-date the Roman era. The name, which means 'Tears of Christ', comes from a myth that Christ, weeping over Lucifer's fall from heaven, spilled his tears on the land and gave divine inspiration to the vines that grew there.

QUICK BREAK
Stop off at **Sorrentino Vini** (sorrentinovini.com; 8am-8pm Mon-Sat) for a wine-tasting tour or overnight stay in their sky-high inn.

★ WORTH A TRIP

Herculaneum (Ercolano)

Though slightly less well known than Pompeii, the seaside ruins of Herculaneum have some of the most well preserved ruins in the entire region. Located on the western side of Vesuvius and much smaller than Pompeii, you can easily visit it in a few hours.

PLANNING TIP
Dogs are welcome in the Archaeological Park of Herculaneum without restriction of breed or size, and the site is free on the first Sunday of every month.

Scan to visit the website for tickets.

Nobles and Gods

Two-storey villa, **La Casa dei Cervi**, overlooked the sea and belonged to a noble family with a twisted sense of humour: cross the lush courtyard to find marble statues of deer being attacked by dogs, and one of a drunkenly inappropriate Hercules. Rich people are just like us!

Built in the 2nd century BCE by the Samnites, who had conquered the Greeks in 421 BCE, **La Casa Sannitica** is a portal into Herculaneum's pre-Roman past. Nearly 300 years old in 79 CE, it had already been renovated numerous times. Some of its unique features include wooden latticework fences on the second storey, an *impluvium* (marble basin to collect rainwater) and a large fresco depicting the rape of Europa.

Casa del Tramezzo di Legno, a double-atrium dwelling, yields the spectacular, if slightly charred, treasures of a large, folding wooden 'privacy' screen and the remains of a wooden bed frame. The partition featured profiled panels and supports for hanging oil lamps, and separated one of the atriums from the common room, which was most likely used to conduct business.

SEAN PAVONE/SHUTTERSTOCK ©

Seaside Ruins and Baths

The vaulted caves that open onto **L'Antica Spiaggia** were most likely used as port warehouses and storage, but after the eruption they became a refuge for those attempting to escape the blast. In 1980 approximately 300 human skeletons were found here, along with necklaces and coins. After decades of painstaking restoration, the beach is now open to the public, and it appears almost as it would have been before the eruption.

**QUICK BREAK
Viva Lo Re**
(vivalore.it)
has great food, amazing service, and a B&B above the restaurant in case you decide that life on the 'golden mile' might just be for you.

Two years after the beach discoveries, archaeologists uncovered the keel of a wooden boat, **Il Gozzo**, very likely used by the victims in a futile attempt to flee. The boat is over 9m long and displayed in the pavilion adjacent to the ruins.

The 1st-century-BCE Terme Suburbane is one of the oldest-known Roman baths, but the **Terme Centrali**, with its *maschili* (male) and *femminili* (female) sections, is especially notable for its remarkable state of preservation. The lavish bathhouse was outfitted with the customary *tepidarium* (warm bathroom), *caldarium* (room with a hot plunge bath) and *frigidarium* (cold room), as well as large pools and marble tubs. The incredibly intricate black-and-white mosaics – mythological sea creatures in the female baths and geometric patterns in the male baths – are nearly intact.

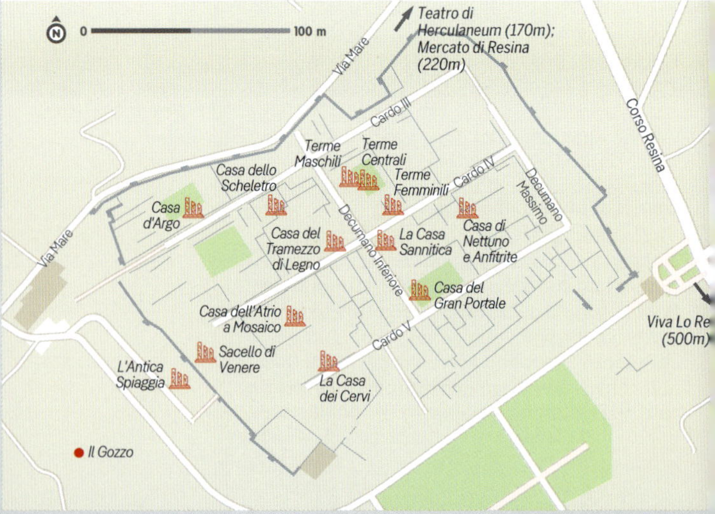

Frescoes and Mosaics

Extraordinary ancient art abounds at Herculaneum. Mosaics like the intricate shrine in the **Casa dello Scheletro**, or the strikingly vivid depiction of Neptune and Aphrodite in the **Casa di Nettuno e Anfitrite**, or the floral and geometric mosaics covering the floor in **Casa dell'Atrio a Mosaico** would be incredible if they were created today, let alone two millennia ago. The frescoes are just as amazing, whether it's those of Hercules at battle on the walls of the **Casa d'Argo**, the stunning brick lintel entrance festooned with birds and bizarre designs in the **Casa del Gran Portale**, or the temple dedicated to Venus in the **Sacello di Venere**.

Both Herculaneum and Pompeii stood for centuries before the eruption of Vesuvius, and they have much more to offer than a snapshot of their tragic demise. Art is what reminds us of the lives that were lived here, and what was celebrated for centuries.

The Theatre

The ancient **Teatro di Herculaneum** was the first monument discovered at what would become this vast archaeological site, but it was discovered by an unassuming farmer named Enzechetta trying to dig a well rather than a team of 18th-century archaeologists. But it wasn't long before they descended and when they began digging they found a 2500-seat auditorium dating from the time of Caesar Augustus with inscriptions to wealthy benefactors, stage doors and columns, and VIP areas. No word on whether old Enzechetta ever got his well, but his discovery set off a race to unearth the ancient city. You can only visit the theatre with a guided tour (€5) that you can book through the website, but it's well worth doing.

VINTAGE FINDS

At the end of WWII, many departing American soldiers would leave their supplies behind in Ercolano and before long, a booming secondhand market emerged. The **Mercato di Resina** became famous, and there are still tons of vintage shops along the Corso Resina. Plus, Piazza Capracotta is still host to the largest sculpture made of jeans that you'll ever see.

★ WORTH A TRIP

Reggia di Caserta

Commissioned by Charles VII in 1752 to rival Versailles, the Reggia di Caserta is a testament to the lengths that rich people will go to better each other. And while you're in Caserta, how about sampling the two best pizzas in the world?

PLANNING TIP
The Reggia is free to enter on the first Sunday of the month, but you must book tickets through the Ticketone platform on the website.

The Royal Palace

The 123-hectare **Royal Palace** is so utterly grand that it's almost impossible to take it all in with only two eyes. You might not see all four courtyards, 1200 rooms and 1790 windows but try your best, starting at the massive central arcade known as the Cannocchiale. Though the Throne Hall was the last to be completed, it is perhaps the most emblematic of the spirit of the palace. The centre of the palace is dominated by the Alexander Hall, named for Alexander the Great because Charles really rooted for an underdog. Leave yourself at least two hours to properly visit.

The Royal Park and English Gardens

Inspired by Versailles in France and the Royal Palace of La Granja de San Ildefonso in Spain, the **Royal Park** is equally monumental. The Bosco Vecchio is home to the Peschiera Grande lake and the Castelluccia is a miniature fortified castle, transformed into a post-hunting rest spot for royal guests. The fountains are fed by the purpose-built Caroline Aqueduct, with deliriously enchanting depictions of Greek gods, goddesses, and mythical creatures that seem to glide on the central Via Acqua that runs the length of the park. This leads to the **English Gardens**, a masterful work

Consult the website for tickets and services.

PARADISE AT RISK/SHUTTERSTOCK ©

undertaken under the guidance of 18th-century botanist John Andrew Graefer.

The World's Best Pizza

Caserta is home to two of the top 10 pizzas in the world, and each is within walking distance from the Royal Palace. Oh, and they're also run by two brothers, which must make Christmas dinners awkward (and delicious). **I Masanielli di Francesco Martucci** *(pizzeriaimasanielli.it)* serves surreal combos and tested classics alongside an admirable natural wine list, while just across town **Sasà Martucci I Masanielli** *(sasaimasanielli.it)* offers an unctuous selection of local favourites paired with regional wines. Both are wildly popular so reservations are recommended, but you could always try one for lunch and the other for dinner.

QUICK BREAK
There is a decent cafeteria and restaurant on the grounds but come on, you're bookending your visit with pizza from the Martuccis, right?

Explore
Capri Town & the Isle of Capri

Despite the hordes that flock here, Capri remains a dream from which few would ever want to wake. Elegant villas dripping with wisteria and bougainvillea perch on steep cliffs that rise majestically from a sapphire sea at the very point where the Gulfs of Naples and Salerno meet. You'll need to be strategic if you want to sidestep the day trippers and content creators, but your efforts are handsomely rewarded.

The tiny pedestrian streets of Capri Town, lined with whitewashed stone buildings, chic restaurants and high-end boutiques, are a delightful maze to wander. Beyond them, rugged yet peaceful trails lead everywhere from ancient ruins to sublime vistas. So bring your stilettos but don't forget your hiking boots because this is an island with many faces.

Getting Around

 Bus

ATC buses and the funicular run from Marina Grande to Capri Town (€2.40 at the booth, €2.90 on board). Buses go to Anacapri but are run by separate companies and tickets are not interchangeable.

 Taxi

Taxi fares are exorbitant and driving is very difficult, so memorise the bus schedule!

THE BEST

ICONIC ACTIVITY Grotta Azzurra (p112)

ISLAND WALK Via del Pizzolungo (p111)

LEGENDARY VIEW Isole Faraglioni (p113)

DIZZYING PANORAMA Monte Solaro (p113)

PEOPLE WATCHING La Piazzetta (p111)

Marina Grande, Isle of Capri
IRYNA SHPULAK/SHUTTERSTOCK ©

★ TOP EXPERIENCE

Capri's Historic Villas

From scandal-riddled Roman emperors and exiled French poets to an enlightened Swedish medic, Capri's high-profile residents have helped shape the island's mythology and solidify its legendary status. And there's no better way to get a sense of their stories than to make the trek up to the villas that became their refuge.

MAP P106 **H1** & **D1**

PLANNING TIP
The villas are only accessible by foot from the town centre, and though the road is paved, make no mistake, these are 40-minute uphill urban treks. Make sure you've got good shoes!

Check out the website for tickets to Villa Jovis.

Villa Jovis

Villa Jovis *(€6)* was the grandest of 12 Roman villas commissioned by Roman Emperor Tiberius (14–37 CE) on Capri, and his main island residence. The ruins recall the emperor's famously debauched proclivities, including imperial quarters and extensive bathing areas in dense gardens and woodland.

The villa's spectacular location posed major headaches for Tiberius' architects. The main problem was collecting and storing enough water to supply the villa's baths and 3000-sq-metre gardens. Their solution was a complex canal system that transported rainwater to four giant storage tanks, whose remains you can still see today.

Beside the ticket office is the 330m-high **Salto di Tiberio** (Tiberius' Leap), a sheer cliff from where, as the story goes, Tiberius had out-of-favour subjects hurled into the sea. True or not, the stunning views are real enough; if you suffer from vertigo, tread carefully.

Villa San Michele

The former home of Swedish doctor, psychiatrist and animal-rights advocate Axel Munthe, **Villa**

TRABANTOS/SHUTTERSTOCK ©

San Michele (*villasanmichele.eu; €10;* pictured) is a must for any itinerary. Built on the site of the ruins of a Roman villa in Anacapri, this early 20th-century complex is perfectly preserved, from its grand sitting rooms to its neoclassical gardens. Take a stroll through the gardens with pathways flanked by immaculate flowerbeds and take in superb views of the Gulf. Just outside the villa you'll find the Scala Fenicia, a stone staircase chiselled by the ancient Greeks that links Anacapri to Capri's Marina Grande.

The villa is an easy 350m walk northeast of Piazza Vittoria in Anacapri, along Via Capodimonte (which becomes Via Axel Munthe).

QUICK BREAK
On the path up to Villa Jovis, down-to-earth **Lo Sfizio** serves typical regional dishes, from pizza and handmade pasta to grilled meats and baked fish.

WALKING TOUR

Walk the Arco Narturale

There's much more to Capri than glamourous shops and chic cafes. Discover the natural beauty of an island that's attracted emperors and exiles for millennia on an easy walk that you can stretch into a half-day wander.

START	END	LENGTH
La Piazzetta	Belvedere del Pizzolungo	4km; two hours

1 Early Bird Special

Wake up (or get there early) and give **La Piazzetta** a long look before leaving the glam life beyond. While it was once a vegetable and fish market, today it is a pricey spot for people watching. If you're flush grab a cappuccino, but be sure to have water with you!

2 Grand Hotels

Quisisana! *Sit omen in nomine.* (It's name is an omen.) One of the island's most famous hotels, **Grand Hotel Quisisana**, began its life as a hospital for patients with lung ailments. Today it's a reference point for those in the know and one of the best places to see why Capri is synonymous with exceptional.

3 Panoramic Gardens

Rising in a series of flowered terraces, the **Giardini di Augusto** (p112) are an ideal lookout point for breathtaking views out to the Isole Faraglioni, a group of three limestone stacks rising out of the sea. The juxtaposition between the manicured gardens and the wild cliffs in front of you is a perfect metaphor for Capri itself.

4 Cliffside Charterhouses

The **Certosa San Giacomo** (charterhouse), built in 1371 by Count Giacomo Arcucci on land donated by Queen Giovanna I of Angiò, is one of the oldest buildings on the island. Today, it houses 17th-century frescoes in its church along with revolving modern art exhibits. From here on, it's all natural beauty.

5 Golden Arches

Dating back to the Paleolithic era and formed by millennia of natural wear and tear, the **Arco Naturale** (natural arch) measures 12m in width and 20m in height. A small terrace by the arch offers views across to Punta Campanella and the Li Galli archipelago.

6 Celestial Caves

Once a temple to Mithra and later a nymphaeum dedicated to the goddess Cybele, the **Grotta di Matermània** still has traces of a mosaic wall and glimpses of the Mediterranean through lush vegetation.

7 Sublime Strolls

Via del Pizzolungo is one of Capri's most beautiful walks, where you'll pass through a much less populated part of the island. From **Belvedere del Pizzolungo** enjoy views of Punta Campanella. That incredible looking villa near the sea below is Casa Malaparte.

8 Awe-Inspiring Viewpoints

The **Punta di Tragara** is one of the best places to look out over the Faraglioni, and if you manage to make it here for sunset or better yet, a full moon, you'll be rewarded with mythical panoramas over the sea. Whenever you go, however, you'll note one thing: in Capri, the best things can indeed be free.

EXPERIENCES

Dive into the Blue Grotto
NATURAL SITE

MAP: ① P106 B1

The famous **Grotta Azzurra** (Blue Grotto) is an illuminated sea cave that's been an object of fascination and worship since ancient Rome. Evidence says that the cave sank by up to 20m in the prehistoric era, leaving only a 1.3m-high entrance. Sunlight is refracted through a small underwater aperture and combines with the reflection of light off the seafloor, producing the vivid blue effect for which the cave is named. But you know all of that.

The easiest way to visit is via a boat tour from Marina Grande, then boarding a row boat into the cave (each paid separately). The crowds, long waiting times, and tip-hungry rowboat operators can be taxing, and you'll only spend about 10 minutes inside the grotto. It's also closed during rough seas and swimming is forbidden. Disclaimers aside, if you get it just right, the Grotta Azzurra is truly a sight to behold.

Stop and Smell the Flowers
GARDEN

The **Giardini di Augusto** (MAP: ② P106 F6) is a short distance from Capri Town and one of the island's most peaceful spots. The panoramic terrace garden is replete with busts, flowerbeds, red-brick trails and a lookout point with soaring views of Marina Piccola and the Faraglioni. Time your visit for the spring bloom for a particularly beautiful experience.

On your way, you'll pass the flagship **Carthusia I Profumi di Capri** (MAP: ③ P106 F5; *carthusia.it*), the current seat of one of Italy's oldest perfume houses, founded in 1380. It's worth a stop just to look at the fairy-tale storefront and get a whiff of the blossoms surrounding it.

Just outside the gardens, you'll find the entrance to the recently reopened **Via Krupp** (MAP: ④ P106 F6), a 1.5km paved hairpin path leading down to Marina Piccola. Closed since 1976 due to safety concerns, Via Krupp once again affords visitors a gentle urban hike with incredible views of the Gulf of Salerno, culminating in a refreshing dip in the sea. And don't worry, the bus will take you back up.

Wander through Capri Town
CITY WALK

Capri Town's beauty is so iconic that it's no wonder most people flock here. Whitewashed labyrinthine streets that show glimpses of tiled courtyards behind hand-painted ceramic street signs under the graceful shade of bougainvillea are as close as you'll get to a quintessential Italian dreamscape.

Capri Town's beating heart is **Piazza Umberto I** (MAP: ⑤ P106 F4), called La Piazzetta by locals.

Once a fish and vegetable market, it's now the best spot for people watching, and don't be surprised if you spot some celebrity faces. Front-row seats don't come cheap, and an espresso can set you back €8 at one of the bars. Further afield towards Via Vittorio Emanuele, a long queue leads to **Gelateria Buonacore** (MAP: 6 P106 F4), a gelateria and pastry shop famous for its *a la minute* (freshly made) pressed waffle cones. Continue to Via Camerelle, Capri's haute couture highway where you'll find the ruins of 40 ancient Roman cisterns. It's easy to get caught up in glamour around here: after all, they've been doing it well for millennia.

Take on Monte Solaro MOUNTAIN

Just off Anacapri's city centre is the entrance to the **chairlift** (MAP: 7 P106 D2; *montesolarocapri.it; one-way/return €11/14*), at Piazza Vittoria, which will whisk you up to **Monte Solaro** (MAP: 8 P106 D3), Capri's highest peak. The 13-minute 589m ride up will provide unforgettable views of terraced vineyards, white houses and lemon groves. On a good day, the Gulf and the Amalfi Coast glimmer in the distance, giving you a sense of what it must have looked like centuries ago.

If vertigo means that minutes feel like years to you, get to the top on foot by following Via Axel Munthe to Via Salita per il Solaro. Go right, then look for the iron crucifix marking La Crocetta pass. A left turn will take you to the hermitage of Santa Maria a Cetrella overlooking Marina Piccola; turning right will get you to the summit. The hike takes about an hour each way. Ride up and walk down, or walk both ways. Keep an eye out for mountain goats, who are often perched at angles that may make you dizzy.

STAND IN AWE AT THE MYTHICAL FARAGLIONI

The **Isole Faraglioni** (MAP: 9 P106 G3) is formed by three stacked crags just off the island's coast: the 109m high Saetta; Stella with its 60m long central cavity; and Scopolo, home of the blue lizard, native only to Capri. Lovers often kiss for luck as they sail through Stella's cavity, probably unaware of most legends. Because the Faraglioni, like many natural wonders in Campania, are linked to Greek myth and not in a good way. Homer believed they were boulders hurled at Ulysses by the Cyclops Polyphemus. Virgil thought they were the legendary home of murderous mermaids, waiting to lure sailors to death. Fun!

LISTINGS

Best Places for...

€ Budget €€ Midrange €€€ Top End

See p106 for map of locations

Eating

Budget Friendly

Salumeria Aldo €
⑩ E2

A Capri classic. This minimart at the port has a delicatessen where you can get a freshly made panino for the perfect beach lunch. *7am-9pm*

Calamore €
⑪ E4

Gourmet fish burger spot that also serves reasonably priced platters of *crudo* (raw seafood). *10am-4.30pm*

Caffe' Manari €
⑫ F4

A coffee bar that serves excellent pastries as well as delicious takeaway pastas, pizzas, panini and fried foods. *7am-9pm Mon-Sat, from 8.30am Sun*

Worth a Splurge

Pescheria Le Botteghe €€€
⑬ F4

Fish market and chic seafood restaurant serving *crudo*, fish burgers, seafood pastas and more. *8am-1pm Mon, 8am-3pm & 7-11pm Tue-Sun*

Lo Zaffiro €€€
⑭ F4

Fancy restaurant serving eclectic 'new' Mediterranean seafood fare with an excellent *cantina* (wine cellar). *noon-3.30pm & 6.30pm-1am*

Gennaro Amitrano €€€
⑮ E3

Michelin-starred seafood restaurant helmed by chef Gennaro Amitrano at Marina Piccola. Elegant farm-to-table fare. *12.30-2.30pm & 7.30-10.30pm*

La Capannina €€€
⑯ F4

A Capri institution since 1931, this boisterous family-run traditional restaurant is touristy, but worth it. Book ahead. *noon-3pm & 7-11.30pm*

Anacapri Budget Eats

Capri Cakes €
⑰ C2

Pastry shop and *tavola calda* ('hot table') serving wonderful *cornetti* (croissants), tasty takeaway panini and pasta, and *aperitivi*. *7am-11.30pm Mon, to midnight Tue-Sun*

Snack Bar da Antonio €
⑱ A4

Unassuming *lido* (beach bar) at Spiaggia del Faro offering panini and gelato. The *caponata* (sweet-and-sour vegetable salad) is a delicious and refreshing treat. *5.45am-9pm*

Aumm Aumm €
⑲ C2

Terrific old-school pizza joint and restaurant just outside Anacapri's centre. Pizzas, fantastic seafood pastas and a large lemon grove to dine in. *noon-3pm & 6.30-11pm*

Sit Down in Anacapri

Trattoria il Solitario €€
⑳ C2

Sprawling, family-friendly restaurant that serves high-quality local favourites in a tranquil garden setting. *noon-11pm*

Ristorante La Zagara €€€
 C2

An elegant restaurant inside a lemon grove, serving light and delicious creative Italian cuisine. The neighbouring, affiliated *vinoteca* (wine shop) has gourmet *aperitivi*. *noon-3pm & 7-11pm*

La Terrazza di Lucullo €€€
 D1

Upscale restaurant serving inventive gourmet Italian fare made with ingredients cultivated in the hotel's clifftop kitchen garden. Spellbinding panoramic Gulf views. *12.30-2.30pm & 7.30-10.30pm*

Drinking

Capri Watering Holes

Giardino Mediterraneo
 E4

Chic outdoor cocktail lounge in a historic lemon grove. Tranquil views and lemon cocktails made with the property's own fruit. *10am-midnight*

Bianca by La Palma
 F4

Luxe cocktail lounge in La Palma hotel, with bespoke cocktails, a restaurant and a rooftop view. 'Island chic' dress code. *6.30pm-1am*

Taverna Anema e Core
 F4

Bar with live music, DJ sets and a full menu of cocktails on Via Sella Orta. No dress code. A Capri institution. *11pm-4.30am*

Hangout Capri
 F4

Capri Town's only gastropub, serving steaks plus classic and inventive cocktails in a cool yet relaxed atmosphere. *hours vary*

A Night Out in Anacapri

Bar degli Artisti
 D1

Swish cocktails and luxe artsy setting in the Jumeriah Palace Hotel. *9am-1am*

The Terrace Bar at Hotel Caesar Augustus
see D1

The sunsets seen from this historic hotel's sweeping clifftop Terrace Bar are legendary. *11am-midnight*

Il Riccio Sea Lounge
see ❶ B1

It may cost a little more than you were hoping but the old school-meets-luxury beach vibes and killer cocktails are worth it. *10am-6pm*

Bar Plaza
 C2

Relaxed, hip bar in the piazza in Anacapri Town with good cocktails and a lively, young *aperitivo* crowd. *10.30am-4am*

Shopping

Capri Town

Yam Capri
㉙ F4

Capri-style clothing with little details that show it cares. *10.30am-9pm*

La Capannina Più
㉚ F4

Wine, chocolate, special preserves and a delicious selection of local treats that you'll definitely want to take home with you. *9.30am-8pm Mon-Sat, 10am-1.30pm & 5-8pm Sun*

Farella Capri
㉛ G4

Luxe artisanal clothing and shawls made exclusively by women for the kind of gift you can only get in Capri. *10am-8pm Mon-Sat, 10am-1pm & 4-8pm Sun*

WALKING TOUR
Walk Procida

Tiny Procida might be the smallest of the three main islands in the Bay of Naples, but there is plenty to explore. Procida is accessible by ferry and hydrofoil; both arrive at Marina Grande and there are multiple connections to Naples with Caremar (40 minutes, eight daily) and SNAV (25 minutes) in high and low season.

START	END	LENGTH
Bar dal Cavaliere	Marina Chiaiolella	5km; two hours

1. Get Your Caffeine Fix

Step off the hydrofoil straight into the portside **Bar dal Cavaliere** where you can get acquainted with Procida's one essential delicacy, the *lingua di bue* – a flaky pastry with a creamy lemon filling. Couple it with a scalding espresso and you're as fuelled as can be for the island ahead.

2. Visit Ghosts

Life here has never strayed too far from Procida's fortified **Terra Murata** (walled town) positioned like an eyrie on the highest part of the island and covered in a coil of narrow, twisting streets that haven't changed much since medieval times. Here you'll find an abbey, a sentinel church, an old palace turned prison, and the ghosts of Procida past.

3. Safe Harbours

Procida's handsomely weathered **Marina Corricella** harbour is more old fishing village than modern mooring, with wooden boats sitting alongside piles of nets and sea breezes fanning lines of drying washing. Populated by tall, warped houses painted in a broad palette of pastel colours, it's a cheerful place full of decent bars and seafood restaurants, and completely free of traffic (cars can't enter).

4. Stealthy Swims

With its weather-beaten jetty, ocean-embracing seafood restaurant and views of Marina Corricella piled on a cliff in the distance, the long narrow beach of **Spiaggia di Chiaia** has a loyal local following. Enter via a 'secret' stairway (or sail in), order a pile of grilled and fried fish in La Conchiglia, and let the waves lull you into an afternoon siesta.

5. Sleepy Squares

The centre of the island and the centre of everyday life on sleepy Procida, the diminutive road junction **Piazza Olmo** is a good place to take pot luck and wander down a narrow lane to see where it takes you (to the sea within 15 minutes). Dented vespas lean against paint-peeled buildings and elderly residents gossip in shop doorways.

6. Charming Coves

Procida's 'third' marina, **Marina Chiaiolella**, is the furthest from the port and is thus less frequented by visitors. Set in a sheltered bay (an extinct volcanic crater), it preserves the air of a self-contained fishing village with its church, main street and array of good restaurants. Stroll through the Santa Margherita neighbourhood to the south for a view of the Isola di Vivara nature reserve.

EXPLORE WALK PROCIDA

See p137 for eating, drinking and shopping listings

Explore
The Amalfi Coast & Sorrento Peninsula

If you're looking for a secret corner of paradise, you're centuries too late to the Amalfi Coast. But who cares?

But first, geography. The Sorrento Coast runs south of Naples from Vico Equense to Massa Lubrense and ends at Punta Campanella. Head east and the Amalfi Coast begins, stretching from Nerano to Vietri sul Mare. It's dense and almost innavigable. But who cares?

For, if you plan well, you'll make cheese in Vico Equense and swim on a beach fit for a queen outside Sorrento. You'll create ceramics in Vietri sul Mare, learn the ancient art of *colatura* in Cetara, and summit the Amalfi Coast at Santa Maria dei Monti. And if you must see Positano with your own eyes, there's a plan for that too. It'll be crowded. But who cares? It is majestic.

Getting Around

 Train
Circumvesuviana trains run to Sorrento from Naples and stop at all five towns on the peninsula.

 Bus
SITA Sud buses are the connective tissue of the Amalfi Coast, and while infuriating at times, they'll serve you well.

 Boat
Sorrento connects to Capri and Positano, but the main ferries for the coast go to and from Salerno from March to October.

Positano (p130)
MACIEJ MATLAK/SHUTTERSTOCK ©

★
THE BEST

HEAVENLY HIKE The Path of the Gods (Sentiero degli Dei; p122)

LEMONY TICKET Amalfi Lemon Experience (p133)

GOURMET GETAWAY Vico Equense (p132)

CRAFTY DAY TRIP Vietri sul Mare (p134)

POSTCARD VIEWS Positano (p130)

For more see

- Top Experiences ⭐ p122
- Experiences 🌟 p132
- Eating ❌ p137
- Drinking ☕ p138
- Shopping 🛍 p139

THE AMALFI COAST & SORRENTO PENINSULA

★ **TOP EXPERIENCE**

The Path of the Gods

Never let it be said that the Amalfi Coast doesn't know about branding. Sometime in the 1980s, enterprising hikers christened an ancient shepherd's trail as something that could have only been called divine. And the Path of the Gods (Sentiero degli Dei) was born.

MAP P120 **E4**

PLANNING TIP
If you packed lightly you can rent hiking boots in Bomerano at **Magici Sentieri** and load up on any other hiking supplies you might need.

Getting Prepared

The **Sentiero degli Dei** is about 6km long each way – starting in Agerola (Bomerano) and ending in the hamlet of Nocelle, just above Positano. Dedicate three to five hours for it, depending on your comfort level and preparation. Keep in mind that it's a moderately challenging hike and not everyone will finish.

Getting There

There are several godly paths to take. The most common way is via bus from Amalfi to Bomerano. From there, hike to Nocelle, and then either take public transportation back to your starting point or continue to Positano. This makes it a mostly downhill walk, which is probably the most logical route for most people. You certainly won't want to reverse the order unless you're missing quad and glute day: it's about 1700 steps up. Besides, then you can celebrate finishing at the lemon slushie stand in Nocelle, which is a win on its own (plus, bathrooms).

Consider a Guide

The Sentiero is well signposted but it's worth getting a guide who will explain the surrounding area to you and make sure you get there and back OK. If you search online there are tons, but make sure they're members of CAI (Club Alpino Italiano).

Get information on the hike from the CAI website.

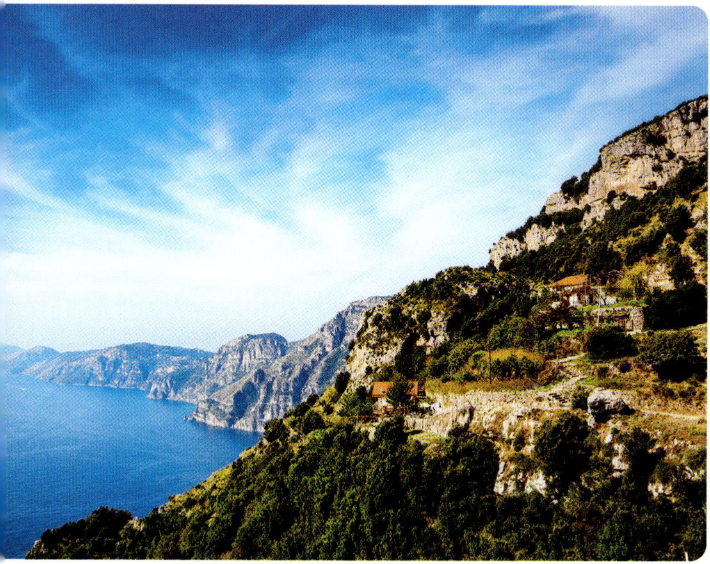

NELLA/SHUTTERSTOCK ©

Supplies are essential: good shoes, water and backpack with a windcheater. Every year people are injured (or worse) and the trail gets very crowded in the high season.

Safety First

If you have a fear of heights, be aware that there are a few sections where the trail runs along the edge of a cliff. Take trail #327a towards Nocelle instead of #327 – you might miss some of the more famous views but you'll feel better.

Also, the earlier you start, the better. You'll find fewer people on the bus and slightly cooler temperatures (especially in the summer).

If you have any emergencies along the hike, dial 118 and give the operator your location using the number on the closest tile that lines the route.

QUICK BREAK
Most people will pack a lunch but for a well-earned lemonade or gelato, the **Chiosco sul Sentiero degli Dei** is a welcome sight.

★ **TOP EXPERIENCE**

Ravello

It cured Richard Wagner's creative block and impressed American writer Gore Vidal enough to stay for 30 years. Ravello, founded in the 5th century as a sanctuary from barbarian invaders fresh from sacking Rome, is the Amalfi Coast's most illustrious hilltop town. It may just be the site of your own metamorphosis.

MAP P120 **F3**

PLANNING TIP The **amico shuttle** (amicoshuttle. com/en/) has round-trip service (€15) to and from Amalfi that you can prebook to save yourself the hassle of queuing for the SITA bus.

Scan for practical information.

Dreamy Villas

The sprawling **Villa Rufolo** (pictured), just off Ravello's Piazza Duomo, is named after the noble family who founded it in the 13th century. In its 700 years, it's also been the residence of King Robert of Anjou, as well as several popes. You can see its history: the 14th-century entrance tower, the Gothic gateway, the curlicued Moorish courtyard, and the 19th-century cascading gardens and lavish sitting rooms with sweeping views of the Gulf. It's not hard to see what inspired Wagner in his opera *Parsifal*.

Just 10 minutes away, **Villa Cimbrone** is a must for anyone in search of a picture-perfect moment. Like Villa Rufolo, it's a medieval structure peppered with influences from subsequent eras, but Villa Cimbrone's major draw is its gorgeous garden. Allow yourself to be transported when you pass through its rose bushes or underneath its leafy pergola, lush with purple blooms. Linger on the Terrace of Infinity, 280m above sea level, with its garden of marble busts and gasp-worthy views.

Both villas also happen to be fancy hotels with frescoed ceilings and Vietri tile floors, so if you're looking for a splash out you could do worse. But even if you can't quite swing a night there, you can enjoy a drink at Villa Cimbrone's Grotto di Eva hilltop garden bar.

THE AMALFI COAST & SORRENTO PENINSULA

EXPLORE

QUICK BREAK

With spectacular terrace views, **Da Salvatore** creates dishes with flair and flavour. Wood-fired pizzas are available in the evenings. Deli-cafe **Babel** offers affordable Italian tapas-style dishes, creative salads and excellent local wines.

An Inspirational Festival

Wagner isn't the only musician to catch inspiration in Ravello. The city quickly became a muse for major 19th- and 20th-century artists who travelled here on their Grand Tours, earning Ravello the title 'City of Music'. It has only become more popular over the years and since 1953, the **Ravello Festival** *(ravellofestival.info)* has showcased world-famous talent from every genre. Each summer the city turns into a stage, with various events unfolding in Piazza Duomo, the cliffside Oscar Niemeyer Auditorium, Villa Rufolo and the streets of the *centro storico*.

Performances begin in early summer and stretch to late July, ranging from orchestral concerts to film screenings. Each year, the festival concludes with cacophonous fireworks in Piazza

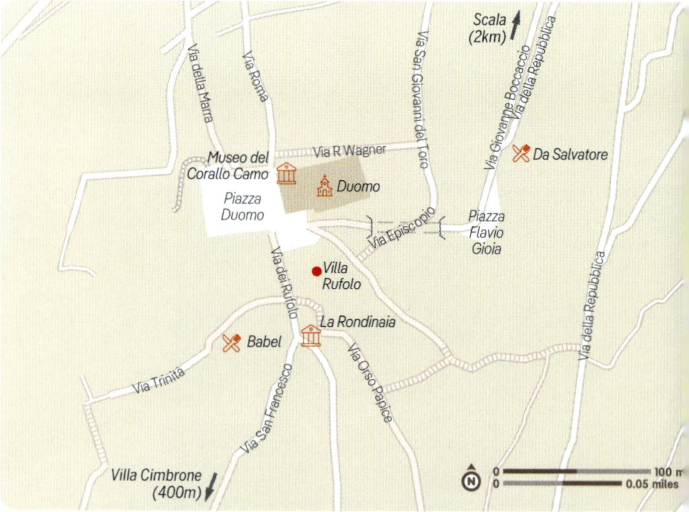

Duomo, with onlookers crammed onto the steps of the cathedral. Check the calendar if you want to plan your trip to coincide with the festival – and why not? It's not every day you get a front-row seat on the roof of the world.

The Swallow's Nest

One of the most extraordinary locations in Ravello is also one of its most enigmatic: **La Rondinaia** (*'the swallow's nest'; larondinaia.com*) was Gore Vidal's home and retreat for more than 30 years, until he sold it in 2005. Since then it has been lovingly restored and transformed into an events space and private villa for rent, but it occasionally opens to the public for tours. If you're lucky enough to catch a glimpse inside you'll see the writer's study preserved in time, and the sweeping views from his Terrace of Inspiration. Even if you aren't a writer, you'll be moved.

Ravello Rambles

Ravello is the starting point for several walks through the Lattari mountains. If you've got the legs for it, walk down to Minori via picturesque steps, hidden alleys and olive groves, passing the beautiful hamlet of Torello en route. This 2.5km walk kicks off just to the left of Villa Rufolo and takes around 45 minutes. Alternatively, you can head the other way, to Amalfi, via the ancient village of Scala. Once a flourishing religious centre with more than a hundred churches and the oldest settlement on the Amalfi Coast, Scala (2km from Ravello) is now a pocket-sized, sleepy place where the wind whistles through empty streets. In the central square, the Romanesque duomo retains some of its 12th-century solemnity. Ask at the Ravello tourist office for more information on local walks.

MUSEO DEL CORALLO

The **Museo del Corallo Camo** sells engraved coral pieces, and the attached museum includes a mid-16th-century Madonna, a 3rd-century-CE Roman amphora, gorgeous tortoiseshell combs, and some exquisite oil paintings. Camo stands out as a true artisan shop in the centre of Ravello; that said, coral is an endangered resource and one you might want to think carefully about before buying.

WALKING TOUR

Walk the Sorrento Centro Storico

There's much more to Sorrento than meets the eye, and the best way to appreciate it is to wander through the maze of streets in its perennially charming centre. Along the way you'll see patron saints and poets, watch craftspeople ply their ancient trade and meet some of the quirky characters that make this a town worth exploring.

START	END	LENGTH
Vallone dei Mulino	Cuore di Pane	1.5km; 1½ hours

1 Ancient Mills
Start at the edge of town overlooking the haunting **Vallone dei Mulino**, ruins of the ancient wheat mills that fed the whole area and one of the most striking examples of the deep valleys that made Sorrento such a distinctive and strategic location.

2 Literary Living Room
It's a short walk to **Piazza Tasso**, the living room of the city where strangely, the famed poet does not occupy centre stage. Instead, the statue of Sorrento's patron Sant'Antonino stands in the middle of the piazza and Torquato Tasso's effigy is rather tucked away next to the famed Fauno Bar.

3 Local Legends
From Piazza Tasso, head down to the **Basilica di Sant'Antonino** where the relics of the patron saint are kept as well as the bones of a whale said to have swallowed a child who was playing on the beach and was saved by Sant'Antonino.

4 A Cultural Cloister
Once you've had your fill of folklore, head to the **Chiostro di San Francesco**, a layer cake of pagan, Roman and medieval architecture now used for art exhibits and performances. The cloister is one of Sorrento's most picturesque spots and perfect for midday refuge when the sun blazes overhead.

5 A Noble Nook
Heading back through the tangle of tiny streets, make a stop at the **Dominova Seat**, a fresco-covered 14th-century nook that once served as a place for nobles to meet and shoot the breeze.

6 Masters at Work
Don't miss the tiny **Chiesa dei Santi Felice e Baccolo**, which once served as the city's cathedral but is now home to one of Sorrento's *intarsio* (inlaid wood) masters, Giuseppe Rocco. Watch him work in his silent reverie and you'll get a sense of what Sorrento must have been like in the days when woodworkers were legion.

7 Neighbourhood Eats
Finish up your walk at **Cuore di Pane**, a great neighbourhood *gastronomia* (delicatessen) offering products from around the region and a huge welcome to anyone who stops in. Don't be surprised if you get talking with Zia Lucia, who often checks in throughout the day.

Walk Positano at Sunrise

If you really want to see Positano, the best way is to book a place here (if you can afford it) and take advantage of the early mornings before the ferries and buses start arriving. It's a long way up, but the views and tranquillity will be worth it.

START	END	LENGTH
Fornillo Beach	Bar Internazionale	5km; 2½ hours

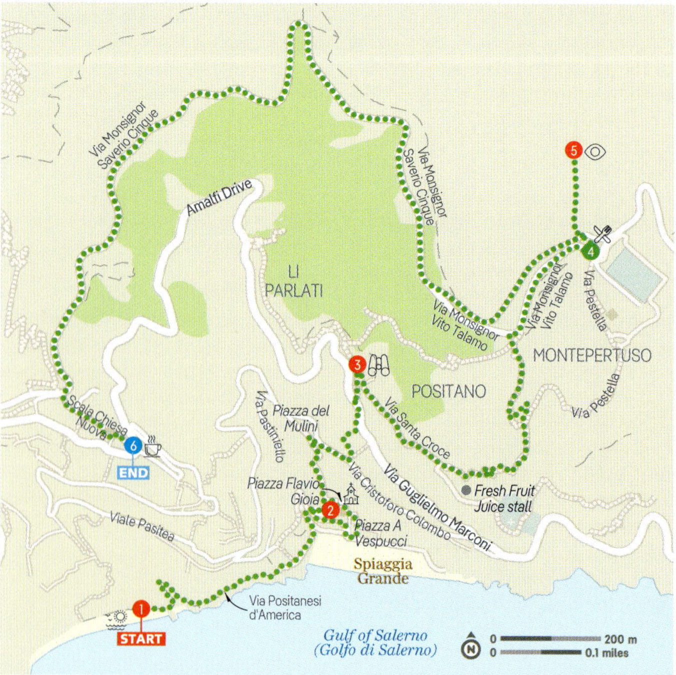

1 Waveside Wakeup

Pack some water and a thermos of coffee and start out from **Fornillo Beach** on the western side of town, a less frequented area that will undoubtedly be quieter even in the early hours of the morning. On the opposite side of the Spiaggia Grande, you'll find people still milling around after Music on the Rocks gets out (they're open until 4am every day), so unless you want to witness some bad decision-making, move along.

2 Ancient Churches

Take the stairs up to the **Chiesa di Santa Maria Assunta**, one of Positano's most famous buildings, which also houses a Byzantine-era Virgin Mary. The hush of the morning is one of the best times to see it as it looks to ancient fishermen at sea. From there, you'll get Via dei Mulini all (or mostly) to yourself, which is the best time to appreciate the latticework holding ancient bougainvillea over your head.

3 Private Panoramas

At the intersection of Via Santa Croce and Via Liparlati, you'll find one of the nicest **panoramas** in town and at that time of the morning, it'll look like you own the place. If you're lucky, the folks running the Fresh Fruit Juice stall along the road will be open, and you'll be able to refresh with an unforgettable lemonade.

4 Romantic Restaurants

Once your thirst is quenched, keep going up Via Santa Croce (and the stairs) until you reach **Donna Rosa**, a family-run restaurant that you'll want to make a note of for your trip back down. From there it's up more stairs but the end is in sight.

5 The Devil's Hole

Legend has it that Mount Gambera was the place where the Devil tried to show his power to the Virgin Mary but failed; instead, Mary touched the Earth at the same point and made a celestial hole right in the middle, known today as **Il Buco di Montepertuso**. As you look through the hole in the rock, watching the sun illuminate the sky, you have proof that a good walk can triumph over evil.

6 Cappuccino Congrats

Take your time making your way back to town and enjoy the gentle slopes and steep staircases that bring Positano's centre back into view. Before you get back to the main drag, however, stop off at the beloved **Bar Internazionale** (p139) for a well earned coffee with the few locals getting ready to start the day.

EXPERIENCES

Go for Secret Swims in Sorrento
BEACH

MAP: **1** P120 **A4**

When original Girlboss Queen Giovanna II of Anjou-Durazzo wanted to get away from the 14th-century hustle and bustle, she'd come down to the dazzling natural pools that formed on the edge of a vast Roman villa just outside of Sorrento. She'd also bring her lovers here for some far-from-prying-eyes frolicking, and legend has it that those who didn't satisfy her rather exacting demands were left to drown.

Although the baths can get crowded in the summer months, they are almost surreal in their beauty and worth the hike to get there. Spend half a day and picnic at the Pollio Felice villa ruins just above the pools. Keep in mind that this is an archaeological site that is said to curse anyone who disrespects it.

Bagni Regina Giovanna is free and only reachable by foot. To get there, take Via Capo from Sorrento to Traversa Punta Capo. Stop into the *alimentari* (grocery store) for a great sandwich and tons of water, then continue down the Traversa until it becomes a footpath that leads to a steep staircase. It's an uneven surface so wear good shoes.

Soak Up Sorrento Street Art
ART GALLERY

MAP: **2** P120 **A2**

Raffaele Celentano is every inch what an artist should be and is exactly the type of person you would have found strolling through Sorrento last century, in search of inspiration. **Gallery Celentano** (*raffaelecelentano.com*), tucked slightly off the main tourist track, is a journey through the city in photos: his scenes of old men playing cards on the street and children grabbing snacks from communal tables are the perfect expression of the peninsula. Have a chat with the artist himself and he'll tell stories of travel and coming home again, many loves lost and found, and the never-ending quest to tell the history of his city. Just across from the gallery in the Vico Secondo Fuoro, Celentano has transformed one of Sorrento's narrow alleyways into an open-air exhibit of photos. It's the perfect place to stumble upon just when you're sure that all hope (or love) is lost.

Hit a Cheesemaking Doubleheader
FOOD

The first official town on the Sorrentine Coast, **Vico Equense** is also home to some of Italy's most famous chefs. If you're looking for a culinary adventure, this is the place.

Vico Equense is also home to cheesemakers who will happily open their doors and invite you to try your hand. **Caseificio Fernando De Gennaro** (MAP: **3** P120 **C3**; *caseificiodegennaro.it*) is the third oldest cheese shop in Italy and has been in the same family since 1850, specialising in Provolone del

Monaco cheese. It has also set up a cheese museum that retraces the entire history of cheesemaking (hint: it's ancient Greek) and can organise either cheese tastings or a demonstration of how it's made. Wine is always included because we are not savages.

Take your skills to the next level with a class at **Caseificio Starace** (MAP: ❹ P120 **C3**) that includes a hands-on mozzarella-making experience that will get you curds deep and ready to knead. You can opt to make the classic *fior di latte* (made with cow's milk), add the chance to churn some fresh butter, or get serious with a *'primo sale'* cheese (the first stage of ageing). Either way, you'll be in good hands and even better company, as the Starace family has been at it for generations.

Head to the Edge of the Earth
NATURAL PARK

MAP: ❺ P120 **A5**

The Greeks called her Athena and the ancient Romans referred to her as Minerva; since the 2nd century BCE, **Punta Campanella Marine Reserve** (*puntacampanella.org*) has been a sacred site dedicated to her. Once you're here, you'll understand why. The expanse of land and sea laid out before your eyes makes it feel like the first time you've ever really used them.

Take the bus from Sorrento or Massa Lubrense toward Termini. It's an easy 8km hike if you want to include a stopover at the San Costanzo Monastery, 486m above sea level. But if you're there for the views, the first 2km is all downhill along the ancient Via Minerva. This Greek-Roman mule track, built in the 4th century BCE, brings you to the Punta Campanella lighthouse. Always look for the red and white symbols painted on rocks. Other hikers or guides will gladly point out the best place to catch the sunset. Give yourself two to three hours to enjoy it.

Fall in Love with Lemons
FARM VISIT

MAP: ❻ P120 **F3**

The **Amalfi Lemon Experience** (*amalfilemonexperience.it*) takes

---

 FIND THE SEA WITHIN

If there is one town of the Sorrentine that truly captures the profound link between land and sea it's the tiny outcrop of Meta, which clings to the cliffs and circles one of the finest coves on the coastline. This is the place where young boys would look out at the deep blue and dream of becoming captains. Indeed the patron saint of Meta, Madonna del Lauro, is a protector of seafarers and her wooden effigy is treasured by the entire peninsula. It's said that if you lend her your ear as she sits on her altar, the Madonna will regale you with tales of great men and even better, good men.

place at the Aceto family farm in the hills above the town, where they've been cultivating the signature citrus since 1825. Guided tours of this organic farm will take you through groves where female workers once carried lemons on their backs, scaling precarious terraces in unimaginable conditions.

Learn from Salvatore Aceto how to make lemon trees stronger and disease-resistant, and how the farm is adapting to climate change. Finish in the cafe and look out onto hushed countryside that feels miles away from crowds and lines. Sign up for the lemon lunch and sample lemon pesto, homemade lemon pastries and 100% organic *limoncello* (lemon liqueur) made in the on-site press. You can also opt for cooking classes or honey tastings, and grab some *limoncello* to take home with you (or have it shipped).

Tours take place throughout the day, and prices vary according to the experience. The meeting point also varies so if you have limited mobility, let Salvatore know and he can assist.

See Amalfi from Above   WALK
MAP: ❼ P120 E3

Santa Maria dei Monti is a plateau on the highest part of the Amalfi coast, and a medium-difficulty day hike will take you through the paths that united the interior of Campania with the coast more than a thousand years ago. While everyone else heads for the Path of the Gods, make your way on this road less travelled.

As you head into the mountains, don't be surprised if the only people sharing the path are shepherds and farmers gathering chestnut wood for Amalfi's signature terraces. When you reach the plateau at 1100m, you'll spot the real treasure of the Amalfi Coast: **Rifugio Santa Maria dei Monti** (*rifugio santamaria.com*) is a shelter run by Antonio Buonaventura, who will prepare a meal for you and has simple but comfortable accommodation in the adjacent lodge. Head over to the panoramic bench he built out of a giant barrel and look down at the silvery waters of the coast. It's quiet, as if in a dream. And just like a dream, you won't want to wake up.

Tour the Town of Ceramics   CITY TOUR

Vietri sul Mare is only a stone's throw from Salerno and though bigger than most of the towns on the coast, is just as charming. However, unlike most Amalfi towns, where fishing was historically the main industry, Vietri has a thriving tradition of ceramic art.

Ceramica Pinto (MAP: ❽ P120 H3; *ceramicapinto.it*) is still in the family palazzo in Vietri centre. Watch the maestri at work on their designs as they look out over the Tyrrhenian Sea. The historic **Ceramica Artistica Solimene** (MAP: ❾ P120 H3; *ceramicasolimene.it*) is also worth a stop if only to enjoy its whimsical exterior, designed by Paolo Soleri in 1951. Overlooking the sea, the kaleidoscopic trims of the Villa Comunale are a perfect example of contemporary Vietri tilework and a central point in town, across from bars, cafes and plenty of people-watching.

Vietri tiles date to the Middle Ages, and a permanent exhibit at the **Museo della Ceramica** (MAP: 10 P120 H3) is dedicated to this art. The museum also hosts concerts and offers incredible views of the town. Free admission, closed Mondays.

Learn the Art of Colatura
COOKING CLASS

MAP: 11 P120 H3

Since the ancient Romans fished these waters, anchovies have been a staple of the Mediterranean diet and the speciality of the tiny town of **Cetara**. But there's much more to this tiny fish than meets the eye: *colatura di alici,* a fish sauce made from the very slow extraction of amber-coloured liquid by the gentle compression of salted anchovies in small chestnut barrels. This is the origin of umami, the very essence of flavour, the essential ingredient that you never knew was inside your favourite dish.

To come to Cetara without gaining an in-depth understanding of *colatura* seems a shame, doesn't it? Luckily, you won't have that problem. Through **Cetara Contadini Pescatori** (cetaracontadini

KNOW YOUR LEMONS!
Campania is synonymous with lemons in all their forms, but each region has its own distinct variety and uses.

Procida lemon
Large and oval-shaped, with a thick, white, spongy rind. The *limone di pane* (bread lemon) is eaten in slices, with or without sugar.

Limone di Sorrento
With high acidity and intense aroma, this is the iconic lemon used in cooking, marmalades and *limoncello*.

Sfusato Amalfitano
This super-sized variety is ideal for sorbets which, in medieval times, were made from snow gathered in the mountains above Amalfi.

pescatori.com; classes per person from €50) programme, you can take part in the experience of making *colatura* with Cetara's famous producers. If you love food experiences or just want to know how things really work, this is a must-do. Classes run from two to six hours for groups of two to 10 people.

Have Your Fill of Wine and Fjords
WINE TASTING

MAP: 12 P120 E4

Furore is called *la città che non c'è* – the city that isn't. There's no centre – just smatterings of buildings decorated with funky murals. But **Cantine Marisa Cuomo** – a female-run winery that's home to multi-award-winning Fiorduva wine, is worth the stop. Tour the hilltop vineyard with views of the sea and the cliffs, or opt for the tasting experience. But don't overindulge – you'll need your wits to climb.

So OK, it wasn't formed by a glacier, but the Furore 'fjord', carved into the rock by the Schiato stream which created a small pebble beach, is iconic. Crowned by an arched bridge, the only way there is down hundreds of stone steps. The 5070 SITA bus from Amalfi is the 'shortest' route; the steps near Cantine Marisa Cuomo take 45 minutes. Nonetheless, the crystal-clear waters and joyous atmosphere are worth it. Furore is a free beach and though it's not as secluded as it once was, it is still a fine way to spend the day.

Head Out to Sea   BOAT TRIP

Family-run **Bluestar Boat Tours** (MAP: ⑬ P120 **C6**; *bluestarpositano. it*) offers a range of tours for every budget and timeframe in Positano. Its early bird and sunset tours offer people a 1½ hour ride around the coast and group tours last all day, while private tours have the flexibility and itinerary you'd expect. The best part? Many of the boats are traditional *gozze*, wooden-hewn fishing boats that define the coast.

Ristorante Da Adolfo (MAP: ⑭ P120 **D4**; *daadolfo.com*) beach club and restaurant is a true Positano throwback. You can only reserve by telephone, and you can only get there in its distinctive red-fish-emblazoned boat. But you'll have the day to hang out on Laurito Beach. Make sure you reserve sun loungers as well as lunch, and enjoy how haphazard it might seem. It would be crazy to promise it won't be crowded, and it's something of a challenge to get exactly right. But it's one of those places that will return to your mind in sepia tones because they just don't make them like that anymore.

 FIND THE TINIEST TOWN

The villages between Amalfi and Salerno have tons of character and each has its own story. Atrani, 600m from Amalfi heading east through the Luna Rossa car park, has the distinct honour of being the smallest town in southern Italy. Its postcard panorama attracted Dutch artist MC Escher in 1923, who took his inspiration for some of his labyrinthine works from Atrani's snaking alleys. It's most recently been the subject of the TV series *Ripley* and you'll find plenty of people looking to retrace those scenes. But then again you'll be on the beach, so no matter.

LISTINGS

Best Places for...

G Budget **GG** Midrange **GGG** Top End

See p120 for map of locations

Eating

Sorrento

Guarracino €€€
 C2
Fresh takes on classics in a former family home that sits perched over the valley. Ask for a table on the terrace. *10am-10pm*

86 Bistro €€€
 B2
A new kid on the block with a working garden right behind the alfresco dining room, and the best mojitos in town. *noon-11.30pm Tue-Sat*

O'Parrucchiano La Favorita €€€
17 B3
It's touristed, it's crowded, and in no way hidden. You'll still beg for a table. *12-3.30pm & 7-10.30pm*

Acqu' e Sale €€
 C1
Seaside seafood and excellent Neapolitan-style pizzas including the local speciality *al limone*, a lemon-flavoured version that will imprint on your palate. *7am-11.30pm*

La Cantinaccia del Popolo €€
 B4
This homely favourite makes a top-notch *spaghetti al pomodoro* (spaghetti with fresh tomatoes), served directly to you in the pan and bursting with flavour. *11am-3pm & 7-11pm Tue-Sun*

On the Sorrento Coast

Torre del Saracino €€€
20 B3
This two-Michelin-starred tower won't be in everyone's budget, but if you're looking for a true splurge Gennaro Esposito is the chef to trust. *12.30-4.30pm & 7.30pm-1am Wed-Sat, 7.30pm-1am Tue, 12.30-4.30pm Sun*

La Salumeria €€
 C3
If you're all about the products, this deli-bistrot in the town centre is the place to get your fill with plenty of local wines to pair. *9am-1.30am*

Don Alfonso 1890 €€€
 B4
A treat in close by Sant'Agata, where ingredients come from Don Alfonso's garden at Punta Campanella. *12.30-2.30pm & 7.30-11pm Wed-Sun Apr-late Oct*

Lo Scoglio €€€
 A5
Celebrities flock in droves but with good reason. You'll never have *spaghetti alla Nerano* (spaghetti with courgettes) this good anywhere else, ever. *12.30-5pm & 7.30-11pm*

Eughenes €€
 A5
Brilliant food, a staff that belongs in a film, and the best backdrop you could imagine. This is movie magic. *1-2.30pm & 8-10pm Fri-Mon*

Amalfi

Trattoria dei Cartari €€
 G4
Head toward the paper museum for a locals-approved meal with the freshest catch in town. *12-3.30pm & 7-10.30pm Tue-Sun*

137

Pizzeria Donna Stella €€

 G4

Set in an atmospheric lemon grove; serves delicious pizza, and salads if you want. *1.30-4pm & 5.30-10pm Wed-Mon, 5.30-10pm Sat & Sun*

Carlo Fiamma €€

 H5

The pizzas are stellar and wines even better from this new kid in town. *noon-midnight*

Ristorante La Caravella €€€

 G6

Splurge-worthy tasting menus that are as much a work of art as the tableaux that adorn the walls and the famous guests that have found their way here. *noon-2.30pm & 7-11pm Wed-Mon*

On the Amalfi Coast

Acquapazza Cetara €€€

see H3

Owner Gennaro Castiello makes his own *colatura* and his own rules, and you'll be glad for both. *1-4pm & 8-11pm Tue-Sun*

Al Convento €€

see 11 H3

Overlooking Cetara's main square, you'll probably see your dinner coming in straight from the sea. *noon-3.30pm & 7-11.30pm Thu-Tue*

Sesta Stazione €€

see H3

The best *pane burro e alici* (bread with butter and anchovy) in Vietri sul Mare. *11am-3.30pm & 6.30-10.30pm Tue-Sun, 6-11pm Mon*

Ristorante 34 da Lucia €€

see 8 H3

Share a table with Vietrese families coming for the catch of the day. *noon-3pm Wed-Mon, 7-11pm Mon & Wed-Sat*

Positano

Casa Mele €€€

 D4

Cool, contemporary restaurant with a lengthy tasting menu and artfully presented food. *7pm-midnight Tue-Sun Apr-Nov*

Next2 €€

 B5

Local and organic ingredients are put to impressive use in dishes such as grilled octopus with baked olives or lamb ravioli with leek and deep-fried artichokes. *6.30-11pm Apr-Oct*

La Cambusa €€€

 D6

Comes with a seafront terrace for those willing to spend for seafood on the beach. *noon-11pm*

C'era Una Volta €€

 B5

Honest, down-to-earth regional grub, including a commendable *gnocchi alla sorrentina* (gnocchi in a tomato and basil sauce) and very fair pizza. *noon-3pm Wed-Mon, 6-11pm daily*

Ristorante il Saraceno d'Oro €€€

 B5

Watch the waiters run across the street with your starters and mains, or better yet, stare off into the horizon with a plate of fresh, local classics. *12.30-3pm & 6.30-11pm Mar-Oct*

Drinking

Aperitivo in Amalfi

Gran Caffè

 H6

The ideal waterfront perch to watch the sun set over the coast. *8am-10pm*

Pansa

35 G6

More than just morning coffee and *cornetti* (croissants), with plenty of non-alcoholic options. *7.30am-11pm*

Masianello Art Cafe
 G6

Hip hangout right outside the port. Makes great margaritas! *11am-2.30am, from 6pm Sun*

Bar della Valle
37 G4

Get away from most of the crowds at this no-frills, super-friendly hangout in the Valley of the Mills. *7.30am-midnight*

Cocktails in Positano

Franco's Bar
38 D6

It would be criminal not to try to get here, even though the prices might magically swallow your wallet. *6pm-midnight*

The Terrace Bar
39 D4

This iconic hilltop in the hotel San Pietro is worth the price tag for those who want sweeping views and classic cocktails. *8am-midnight*

Fly
 D6

Come on, when was the last time you had it large? Start here and continue below at Music on the Rocks. *7pm-1am*

Bar Internazionale
41 B5

The closest you'll get to no frills in town, with locals stopping in for their own *aperitivo*. *7am-11pm Thu-Tue*

Shopping

Amalfi

JP Boutique
42 G5

Signature Amalfi designs, gauzy fabrics and unique accessories from an Amalfi-born artist and illustrator with a flair for the dramatic. *9am-8.30pm*

L'Altra Costiera
43 G5

The best place in Amalfi for locally sourced ceramics from up-and-coming and established artists, many from Vietri sul Mare. *10am-8pm*

La Scuderia del Duca
44 G6

Tucked behind the Terminal restaurant at the port, this place is full of great antiques and funky paper crafts that make excellent gifts. *10am-7pm*

Positano

La Bottega di Brunella
 C5

One of the reasons local women always look so effortlessly chic. *9am-9pm*

Ceramiche Maria Grazia
46 C5

Subtle and sophisticated, with lots of lemons emblazoned onto urns, plates, tables and even egg cups. *9.30am-8.30pm May-Oct*

La Botteguccia de Giovanni
 C5

Craftsman Giovanni creates handmade leather sandals in his small workroom at the back of the shop. *9.30am-9pm May-Oct*

Sorrento

Mastellone
48 B2

This tiny shop is the ideal place to go for modern *intarsio* (inlaid wood) designs that are just as carefully intricate as the classics. *9.30am-10.30pm*

Biagio Barile
49 C2

There's a story behind every piece at this family operation that occupies a former church. *9am-9pm Mon-Fri, 9am-1pm & 4pm-9pm Sat-Sun*

Stinga Tarsia
 C2

Three generations of woodworkers continue the traditions that have made their way onto runways. *9.30am-9.30pm*

Naples & the Amalfi Coast Toolkit

Family Travel	142
Accommodation	143
Food, Drink & Nightlife	144
LGBTIQ+ Travellers	146
Health & Safe Travel	147
Responsible Travel	148
Accessible Travel	150
Nuts & Bolts	151
Language	152

Procida (p116)
BORIS STROUJKO/SHUTTERSTOCK ©

Family Travel

Volcanoes! Roman ruins! Beaches! All the pizza! Gelato to placate tempers! Campania is a dream for families. Whether you've got young kids or want to organise a multigenerational holiday, there's a spot for you.

If Your Child Is Neurodivergent
Italians have a soft spot for kids but they've become particularly attuned to neurodivergent children (still referred to as *autismo*). If you're travelling with children who need more time, different schedules, or anything else to make them comfortable don't hesitate to tell people at restaurants, tours or hotels. Italians are incredibly accepting and accommodating.

EATING OUT
Restaurants don't always have children's menus but they will usually make you something simple for kids on request. Children also stay out with their parents here and that means late hours, so make sure they have those afternoon naps!

Mind the Stairs
When volcanoes are underfoot it takes a lot of stairs to build towns and cities. Let your kids know that they'll be walking and climbing more than usual, and reward them (and yourself) with gelato.

Too Spooky
Museums and archaeological sites contain skeletons, skulls, or other macabre artefacts that might feel a little too real for the youngsters. Prepare them beforehand and don't be afraid to skip it if it gets too intense.

Free for kids
Many museums and archaeological sites are free for children under 18, and that adds up to some serious savings!

Inspiring Activities
There are archaeological sites both above ground and underwater, cooking classes for all ages, and ceramics painting for young artists. Let your children choose their adventures and they might be inspired for a lifetime.

FROM LEFT: OKSANA MIZINA/SHUTTERSTOCK ©, PICS FIVE/SHUTTERSTOCK ©

Accommodation

No matter what your taste (or your budget) there's somewhere in Naples or on the coast that will tick all the boxes.

Where to Stay if You Love...

Being in the Action
Santa Lucia and Chiaia (p77) Boutique hotels, buzzing streets, and easy connections with the coast and Capri make this the spot if you want to make the most of Naples.

Glamming it Up

Capri (p105) You'll spend a pretty penny to find your perch and the high season brings crowds, but there's nothing like waking up to island views over the sapphire sea.

Historic Hospitality
Sorrento (p128) It has got some of the oldest hotels in Italy – though the grandeur comes at a price. Sorrento feels like stepping back in time (with all the mod cons).

Vibrant Street Scenes

Centro Storico (p35) This is the heart of Naples and wake-ups here mean hearing the sounds of people getting their days started, the aroma of fresh espresso, and the distant Sirens' song of the sea.

Neighbourhood Vibes

La Sanità (p65) This once downtrodden area of Naples is one of its most lively, and today you'll find artists and old-timers swapping stories in the local bar. Join in.

OUR PICK

We Love to Stay in...

Toledo (p51) In the heart of the action but with plenty of secret corners for quiet and charming hideaways. Where else can you stay in the middle of a 19th-century shopping mall?

HOW MUCH FOR A NIGHT IN

A B&B in Naples
€75–90

A hotel in Capri (high season)
from €350

A boutique hotel in Chiaia **from €150**

Food, Drink & Nightlife

Allergies and Intolerances

Italy has strict rules that require restaurants to list their ingredients for possible allergens, so this should be available (often in English and Italian). Italians take allergies seriously, so if you do have one let them know when you reserve your table.

HOW TO SAY

I'm allergic to...
Sono allergica/o a...
I am celiac
Sono celiaca/o

HOW TO ASK...

Does this contain nuts?
Questo contiene la frutta secca?
Is this gluten free?
È senza glutine?
Is there a vegan option?
C'è un'opzione vegana?

PACE YOURSELF

Naples is a land of plenty, and when it comes to portions that means abundant sizes. Order a bit at a time and if you're lucky enough to be invited to a family dinner, wear something stretchy!

A Tip on Tips

Tipping is not compulsory in Italy, despite what you may be told in some more heavily touristed locations. If you do feel like leaving something for service, it's usually around 10%. Also, avoid doing the weird palm maneuver. This isn't an '80s movie.

HOW TO... Pay the Bill

Italy has embraced the digital economy so you can pay for just about anything (even a coffee) with a chip-enabled card. Indeed, the law requires that contactless payments be available to customers, so you'll very likely find them even in remote locations. However, many places still struggle with wifi or phone signal so do remember to have a bit of cash on hand should card payments be interrupted. However, tips cannot be added to card payments in Italy so if you're inclined to add something for the staff, that will have to be in cash.

PRICE RANGES
The following refer to the average price for a main course:

€ less than €12
€€ between €13–27
€€€ more than €28

OPENING HOURS
Cafes 7am–8pm
Pizzerias 10am–midnight
Restaurants 12.30pm–3pm & 7.30–11pm

Going Out

Aperitivo An evening out in Naples and the Amalfi Coast will almost certainly start with an *aperitivo* – cocktails and snacks at a *bar* (cafe) or *locale* (bar, pub), preferably in a piazza. *Aperitivi* range from potato chips and neon-green olives to quality *taglieri* (charcuterie) and *fritti* (fried treats). There's been a cocktail movement in the past few years so you'll find all manner of Anglo-style drinks, but the classic spritz, Negroni (pictured), or *calice di prosecco* (glass of prosecco) never fail.

Nightlife Italian nightlife doesn't really begin until midnight so after dinner, head to a *locale* or *discoteca*. There may be a DJ set or a live music set, and you should expect to pay something to get in. You should also look the part, so smart casual is the standard. When it comes to *superalcolici* (spirits), bespoke cocktails are in, and gin is the word.

HOW MUCH FOR A

Espresso
€1

Pizza
€4 and up

Lunch at a trattoria
€15 and up

Dinner (three courses)
€50 and up

Glass of wine
€4 and up

Domestic beer
€3

Spritz
€5 and up

LGBTIQ+ Travellers

Naples and the Amalfi Coast is home a thriving LGBTIQ+ community with a long history of queer culture in art, music and literature.

The Best Spots

There are a number of gay and queer-friendly areas in Naples, particularly Piazza Bellini in Naples' *centro storico,* which is home to several LGBTIQ+ friendly nightspots, like Intra Moenia literary café, Volver and Lemme Lemme. Also try Hotel de Charme, Il tempo del vino e delle rose and Ghetto Crime bar in Chiaia.

What are the islands and the Campania coast without their beaches? There are a number of gay beaches in the area, such as Spiaggia di Cuma in Campi Flegrei. The One Fire Beach Club near Praiano and the Bagni di Regina Giovanna in Sorrento also have gay areas. Capri and Ravello also have a long history of queer artists in residence.

Quiiky *(quiiky.com)* is an Italian LGBTIQ+ friendly travel agency that arranges tours and offers travel deals. Amalfi Coast Guides offers tailormade hikes all over the coast and is proudly LGBTIQ+ friendly.

OUR PICKS

Best for...
PRIDE **Napoli Pride** launched in 2009 and is one of the largest in Italy. Events, concerts, and workshops draw thousands from around the world.
MURALS Check out the **Murales della Tarantina** in the Quartieri Spagnoli, dedicated to the trans performer who was Fellini's muse in the 1950s.
DRAMA **La Rondinaia** in Ravello was Gore Vidal's residence and offers the most incredible views of almost anywhere on the coast.

PLANNING INFO

Information on LGBTIQ+ friendly bars, hotels and activities can be found on websites like Gay Friendly Italy *(gayfriendlyitaly.com),* We Are Gayly Planet *(wearegaylyplanet.com)* and Travel Out *(travelout.it).*

TRANSGENDER SUPPORT

Infotrans provides information and links to services for transgender people, and is sponsored by the Italian Institute for Health.

Resources

- **arcigaynapoli.org** Arcigay is Italy's main LGBTIQ+ organisation. Its website offers a rundown of special events and initiatives held in town and all over Italy. It is dedicated to fighting discrimination and encouraging inclusion.

Health & Safe Travel

From folklore cures to high-tech treatments, there are plenty of resources available to stay healthy.

FARMACIA VS PARAFARMACIA

If you need a prescription filled go to a *farmacia*, but if you're looking for natural cures, homeopathic medicine or cosmetic therapies, find the nearest *parafarmacia*. The first is staffed by pharmacists who can write prescriptions whilst the second will not carry pharmaceutical drugs.

Pharmacy vs Doctor

No one likes getting sick but in Italy, healthcare is readily available and accessible. If your ailment isn't serious, make a *farmacia* (pharmacy) your first stop. The pharmacist can give medical advice and over-the-counter medications, or point you in the right direction if need be. For emergency treatment, the *pronto soccorso* (casualty/the ER) is available; call 118 if you need an ambulance.

Drink the Water!
Unless a sign says *'acqua non potabile'*, all tap water is suitable for drinking.

QUICK INFO

Drugs
Still not legal, don't buy or carry.

Crime
Not as bad as before but still, exercise caution.

Getting Lost
If you're hiking, don't be afraid to ask a guide for help!

Women Travellers

If you're travelling alone or with other women around Naples you might receive attention. While much of it is harmless, your comfort level is paramount: be firm if the attention is unwanted. Italian authorities are very responsive to complaints by female tourists (it's bad for business) so use it to your advantage if needs must.

--- SCAMS ---

Taxis in Naples can overcharge you if you're not watching. Book one through Uber or FreeNow for a fixed rate that you can follow.

Responsible Travel

Naples and the Amalfi Coast are some of the most frequented destinations in the world, and overtourism is a challenge that affects people working in the industry as well as those who live in cities and towns all over the region. Travelling responsibly in these places doesn't mean that you can't go, but it does help to research beforehand.

Meet Family-Run Businesses

Amalfi Lemon Experience (p133) isn't just environmentally sustainable, it's a great example of the generational continuity that helps communities maintain their distinctive identity.

FROM LEFT: PHOTOONGRAPHY/SHUTTERSTOCK ©, MEHANIQ/SHUTTERSTOCK ©

OUR PICK ★

Parco Sommersa di Baia

Learn about the protected marine area and underwater archaeological ruins that are now one of the most studied areas in Italy.

Solutions to Overtourism

Overtourism is a massive challenge in Positano, but family-run companies like **Bluestar Boat Tours** (p136) are part of the solution. Ride aboard a traditional *gozzo* for a unique experience that also keeps one of the most precious cultural resources of the coast alive. And remember, a little kindness in those crowded months goes a long way.

Resources

- **rinnovabili.it** Daily publication about environmental issues in Italy.
- **fondoambiente.it (FAI)** Italy's first stop for all things eco-related, including current initiatives, events and volunteer opportunities.
- **puntacampanella.org** Information about the area's protected waters.

SUSTAINABLE SHOPPING

Buy vintage clothing on **Via Mezzacannone** (p30), a historic street in Naples' University district where traders from the Mercato di Resina would sell their wares. If you're looking for products, locally owned Jamalfi transforms local raw materials – including Amalfi's sfusato lemon – into organic face, hair and body balms. Wherever you are, seek out small, independent producers for souvenirs rather than mass-produced trinkets. After all, we remember the story long after the product is gone.

Support Sustainable Art

Take a tour with **Napoli Paint Stories tour** (p45) to understand why graffiti is so important to the identity of the city, and why preserving it is also a way to make sure that history continues to be written. Or, hang out with **Raffaele Celentano** (p132) at his gallery in Sorrento and support an independent artist with a million stories to tell.

WALK IT OFF

So much of the coast and its cities are accessible only by foot, so take it slow and embrace the stairs. There's no better way to see a place, both for you and the environment.

Climate Change & Travel

It's impossible to ignore the impact we have when travelling; Lonely Planet urges all travellers to engage with their travel carbon footprint, which will mainly come from air travel. While there often isn't an alternative, travellers can look to minimise the number of flights they take, opt for newer aircrafts and use cleaner ground transport, such as trains. One proposed solution – purchasing carbon offsets – unfortunately does not cancel out the impact of individual flights. While most destinations will depend on air travel for the foreseeable future, for now, pursuing ground-based travel where possible is the best course of action.

The **UN Carbon Offset Calculator** shows how flying impacts a household's emissions.

The **ICAO's carbon emissions calculator** allows visitors to analyse the CO_2 generated by point-to-point journeys.

Accessible Travel

A Changing Map

The topography and ancient architecture of Naples, the coast and the islands pose significant challenges for travellers with limited mobility. But improvements are coming – Campania has announced an initiative to remove all architectural barriers to its monuments and a number of the area's beaches are becoming accessible.

Accessible Airports

Naples International Airport provides 45 free accessible parking spaces, platforms with access ramps, paths for the visually impaired plus tactile maps, and traffic lights with sound indications. There are free assistance services; call 48 hours prior to departure.

OUR PICK

The **Archaeological Park of Pompeii** (p90) has unveiled an entire programme of accessibility features, including a more than 3.5km-long itinerary, from the access point of Piazza Anfiteatro to the Sanctuary of Venus, along the main streets of the ancient city. All visitors can now access the most significant buildings and domus, and maps with accessibility points are available on the Pompeii website (pompeiisites.org).

ACCOMMODATION

The newer and larger hotels will have some adapted rooms, but to be sure the standards are up to snuff ask at the local turismo. Many campgrounds have accessible facilities (campeggi.it).

Train Travel

Italy's national rail company, **Trenitalia** (trenitalia.com), offers a helpline and list of accessible stations for passengers with disabilities. To secure assistance at Napoli Centrale, call 24 hours before your trip.

BUS TRAVEL

A growing number of city buses (including the R2 in Naples) now have ramps and a wheelchair space, as well as privileged routes and tactile maps for the blind.

Resources

- **Casamundo** (casamundo.it) Locates accessible holiday accommodation.
- **Turismo Accessibile** (turismoaccessibile.org) Provides a list of accessible hotels, restaurants, beaches and museums.
- **Accessible Italy** (accessibleitaly.com) Specialises in holiday services for people with disabilities.
- **Salablu** (salablu.it) From Trenitalia; finds railway stations that provide assistance services for passengers with disabilities and reduced mobility.
- **Kimap** This app finds the most accessible paths for visitors on wheels.

Nuts & Bolts

Opening Hours

Banks 8.30am–1.30pm and 2.45–3.45pm or 4.15pm

Cafes 7.30am–8pm or later

Clubs 11pm–5am

Post offices 8am–6pm Monday to Friday, 8.30am–1pm Saturday

Restaurants Noon–3pm and 7.30–11pm or midnight

Shops 9am–1pm and 3.30–7.30pm (or 4–8pm)

QUICK INFO
Time Zone Central European Time CET (GMT+2)
Country calling code +39
Emergency number 113
Population 1,054,840

Wifi
Public wifi is readily available at many restaurants and bars.

ELECTRICITY

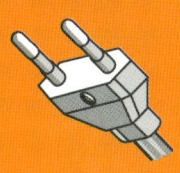

Type C
230V/50Hz

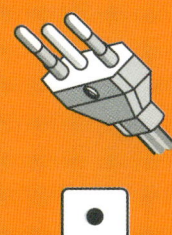

Type L
230V/50Hz

Public Holidays

New Year's Day (Capodanno) 1 January

Epiphany (l'Epifania) 6 January

Easter Monday (Pasquetta) March/April

Liberation Day (Festa della Liberazione) 25 April

Labour Day (Festa dei Lavoratori) 1 May

Republic Day (Festa della Repubblica) 2 June

Feast of the Assumption (l'Assunzione or Ferragosto) 15 August

All Saints' Day (Ognisanti) 1 November

Feast of the Immaculate Conception (Festa dell'Immacolata Concezione) 8 December

Christmas (Natale) 25 December

Boxing Day (Festa di Santo Stefano) 26 December

Aperto Open
Chiuso Closed

Language

Italian Basics

Hello.
Buongiorno.
bwon·*jor*·no

Goodbye.
Arrivederci.
a·ree·ve·*der*·chee

Hi./Bye.
Ciao. chow

Yes./No.
Sì./No. see/no

Please.
Per favore.
per fa·*vo*·re

Thank you.
Grazie. *gra*·tsye

You're welcome.
Prego. *pre*·go

Excuse me.
Mi scusi.
mee *skoo*·zee

Sorry.
Mi dispiace.
mee dees·*pya*·che

Fast Phrases

Do you speak English?
Parla/Parli inglese? (polite/informal) *par*·la/*par*·lee een·*gle*·ze

I don't understand.
Non capisco. non ka·*pee*·sko

I'd like...	**Vorrei...**	vo·*ray*...
a coffee	**un caffè**	oon ka·*fe*
the menu	**il menù**	eel me·*noo*
two beers	**due birre**	*doo*·e *bee*·re
a table (for three people)	**un tavolo (per tre persone)**	oon *ta*·vo·lo per tre per·*so*·ne

The bill, please.
Il conto, per favore. eel *con*·to per fa·*vo*·re

How much is it?
Quanto costa? *kwan*·to *cos*·ta

Could you please speak more slowly?
Può/Puoi parlare più lentamente, per favore?
(pol/inf) pwo/pwoy par·*la*·re pyoo len·ta·*men*·te per fa·*vo*·re

Where's...	**Dov'è...**	do·*ve*...
the station?	**la stazione?**	la sta·*tsyo*·ne
the toilet?	**il bagno?**	eel *ba*·nyo
the nearest ATM?	**il Bancomat più vicino?**	eel *ban*·co·mat pyoo vee·*chee*·no

Could I have a receipt, please?
Può darmi una ricevuta, per favore? pwo *dar*·mee *oo*·na ree·che·*voo*·ta per fa·*vo*·re

Numbers

uno   **due**   **tre**   **quattro**   **cinque**
oo·no   *doo*·e   *tre*   *kwa*·tro   *cheen*·kwe

Good to Know

Most sounds in Italian also exist in English. Remember that **z** sounds like *ts*, **r** is rolled and **c** resembles the English *ch* when it comes before an 'i' or 'e'.

Italian has three words for 'you'. Use the polite form **Lei** *lay* if you're talking to a stranger, an official or someone older than you. With someone familiar to you or younger than you, you can use the informal form **tu** *too*. For a group of people, use **voi** *voy*. The verbs have a different ending for each person, like the English 'I do' vs 'he/she does'.

The useful word **Prego** has several meanings, including 'You're welcome', 'Go ahead' and 'Next, please'.

FALSE FRIENDS

Warning: many Italian words look like English words but have a different meaning altogether, eg **camera** is a room, not a camera (use **macchina fotografica**), and **stampa** is the press or media, not a postage stamp (**francobollo**).

Signs

Entrata/Ingresso Entrance
Uscita Exit
Aperto Open
Chiuso Closed
Informazioni Information
Proibito/Vietato Prohibited
Gabinetti/Servizi Toilets
Uomini Men
Donne Women

Listen for

Il Suo passaporto. eel *soo*·o pa·sa·*por*·to
Your passport.

Il treno è in ritardo/cancellato.
eel *tre*·no e een ree *tar* do/kan·che·*la*·to
The train is delayed/cancelled.

ROMAN SLANG TO LISTEN OUT FOR

Daje! Pronounced '*da*·yeh', this is similar to the English 'Come on!' Hear fans of the capital's two football teams, Roma and Lazio, shouting it from the stands.

Aò! While 'Ciao' is perfectly fine, this is the truly Roman way to say 'Hi'. It can express a range of other sentiments, too, from protest to agreement – it's all about context.

Annamo a magnà. In standard Italian, you'd say 'Andiamo a mangiare' to mean 'Let's go to eat'. Romans don't have the patience for all those syllables.

sei
sei

sette
se·te

otto
o·to

nove
no·ve

dieci
dye·chee

Index

Sights 000   Map pages 000

See also separate subindexes for:
- Eating p157
- Drinking p158
- Shopping p158

accessible travel 29, 150
accommodation 25, 143
activities 16, *see also individual activities*
air travel 26
allergies 144
Amalfi (town) 134, 137-8, 138-9, **120-1**
Amalfi Coast & Sorrento Peninsula, the 119-39, **120-1**
  drinking 138-9
  experiences 122-7, 132-6
  food 137-8
  highlights 122-7
  itineraries 128-9, 130-1, **128, 130**
  shopping 139
  top experiences 122-7
  transport 119
  walking tours 128-9, 130-1, **128, 130**
Amalfi Lemon Experience 8, 133-4, 148
Anfiteatro 90
aperitivo 145
archaeological sites & ruins 12-13, 44, 70, 90-5, 98-101
Arco Naturale 110-11, **110**
area codes 151
arriving 26
art galleries, *see* museums & galleries
Artecard 23, 27
Atrani 136

Bagni Regina Giovanna 16, 132
Basilica di San Francesco di Paola 60
Basilica di San Gennaro Fuori le Mural 69
Basilica di San Severo 69
Basilica di Sant'Antonino 129
beaches 16
Belvedere del Pizzolungo 111
Belvedere di Sant'Antonio a Posillipo 89
Biblioteca Nazionale 55
Bluestar Boat Tours 136, 148
boat travel 26, 28, 136, 148
Borgo Marinaro 84-5
budget 23, 145
bus travel 26, 27, 28
bush walking, *see* hiking
business hours 145, 151

Cantine Marisa Cuomo 8
Capodimonte, *see* La Sanità & Capodimonte
Cappella di San Gennaro 38
Cappella Sansevero 6, 40-1, 43
cappuccino 22
Capri Town & the Isle of Capri 105-15, **106-7**
  drinking 115
  experiences 108-9, 112-13
  food 114-15
  highlights 108-9
  itineraries 110-11, **110**
  shopping 115
  top experiences 108-9
  transport 105
  walking tours 110-11, **110**
car travel 26
Carnevale 24
Casa d'Argo 101
Casa del Gran Portale 101
Casa del Tramezzo di Legno 98
Casa dell'Atrio a Mosaico 101
Casa dello Scheletro 101
Casa del Nettuno e Anfitrite 101
Casa Natale di Totò 71
Caseficio Starace 8
Castel dell'Ovo 30, 81, 85

Catacombe di San Gennaro 17, 70
Centro Storico 35-47, **36-7**
  drinking 46-7
  experiences 38-41, 44-5
  food 46
  highlights 38-41
  itineraries 42-3, **42**
  shopping 47
  top experiences 38-41
  transport 35
  walking tours 42-3, **42**
Certosa e Museo di San Martino 6, 74-5
Certosa San Giacomo 111
Cetara 8, 135
Cetara Contadini Pescatori 135
cheese 8
Chiaia, *see* Santa Lucia & Chiaia
Chiesa dei Santi Felice e Baccolo 129
Chiesa del Gesù Nuovo 43, 44
Chiesa della Certosa 74
Chiesa di San Giovanni a Mare 49
Chiesa di Santa Maria Assunta 131
Chiesa di Santa Maria del Carmine 49
Chiesa di Santa Teresa a Chiaia 81
Chiesa di Sant'Eligio Maggiore 49
Chiesa e Chiostro di San Gregorio Armeno 44
children, travel with 17, 142
Chiostro di San Francesco 129
Chiostro Grande 74
Cimitero delle Fontanelle 30, 70
Circumvesuviana 28
climate 24
cocktails 145

colatura 8, 135
Complesso Monumentale di Santa Chiara 44-5
coral 127
costs 23, 29, 145
courses 133, 134, 135
Cristo Velato 40-1
currency 23

D
dangers 22, 147
disabilities, travellers with 29, 150
Dominova Seat 129
drinking 8-9, 144-5, *see also individual neighbourhoods*, Drinking *subindex*
drinks, *see* cappuccino, cocktails, water, wine
Duomo di Napoli 11, 38-9, 43

E
eating, *see* food, Eating *subindex*
electricity 151
Eleonora Pimentel Fonseca Mural 57
emergencies 151
English Gardens 102
Equation Clock 30, 59
etiquette 22, 60
events 11, 24-5

F
family travel 17, 142
Ferragosto 24
ferry travel 26, 28
Festa di San Gennaro 25
festivals 11, 24-5
food 8-9, 144-5, *see also individual neighbourhoods,* Eating *subindex*
football 11, 30, 54, 84
Fornillo Beach 131
Foro 91, 93
free activities 17
funicular travel 27-8

G
Galleria Borbonica 85
Galleria Umberto I 59
galleries, *see* museums & galleries
Gallery Celentano 132

gay travellers 146, *see also* Napoli Pride
Giardini di Augusto 17, 111, 112
Gran Cono 96
Grand Hotel Quisisana 111
Grotta Azzurra 16, 112
Grotta di Matermània 111

H
health 147
Herculaneum 12, 17, 98-101, **100**
highlights 6-17, *see also individual neighbourhoods*
hiking 14-15, 122-3, 134
holidays 151
Holy Mile, the 68
Horse Riding Tour Naples 96
Hypogeum Gardens 44

I
Il Buco di Montepertuso 131
Il Gozzo 100
Il Lupanare 93
Insula dei Casti Amanti 94
internet resources 146, 148, 150
Ipogeo dei Cristallini 12, 70-1
Isle of Capri, the, *see* Capri Town & the Isle of Capri
Isole Faraglioni 113
Italian 152-3
itineraries 18-21
Capri Town & the Isle of Capri 110-11, **110**
Centro Storico 42-3, **42**
La Sanità 68-9, **68**
Mercato & Borgo Orefici 48-9, **48**
Mergellina 88-9, **88**
Positano 130-1, **130**
Procida 116-17, **116**
Quartieri Spagnoli 56-7, **56**
Santa Lucia & Chiaia 80-1, 82-3, **80, 82**
Sorrento 128-9, **128**

L
La Casa dei Cervi 98
La Casa Sannitica 98
La Chiesa di Santa Maria Maddalena ai Cristallini 30, 69, 71
La Festa del Pesce 25
La Piazzetta 111

La Rondinaia 127
La Sanità & Capodimonte 65-73, **66**
drinking 73
experiences 67, 70-1
food 72-3
highlights 67
itineraries 68-9, **68**
shopping 73
top experiences 67
transport 65
walking tours 68-9, **68**
La Torretta di Mergellina 89
language 152-3
L'Antica Spiaggia 99
Le Luci d'Artista 24
lemons 8, 133-4, 135
LGBTIQ+ travellers 146, *see also* Napoli Pride
Lungomare 85

M
MADRE 6, 45
MANN 6, 58
Mappatella Beach 16, 89
Maradona, Diego 54
Marina Chiaiolella 117
Marina Corricella 117
medical services 147
Mercato & Borgo Orefici 48-9, **48**
Mercato della Pignasecca 8, 57
Mercato di Porta Nolana 17, 49
Mergellina 88-9, **88**
Meta 133
metro 27
money 23
Monte Solaro 14, 113
Mt Vesuvius 14, 96-7
Museo Archaeologico Nazionale di Napoli 58
Museo del Corallo Camo 127
Museo del Tesoro di San Gennaro 38
Museo della Ceramica 6, 135
Museo di Capodimonte 6, 67
Museo Pignatelli 81
museums & galleries 6-7, 59

N
Napoli Centrale 26
Napoli Paint Stories tour 45
Napoli Pride 11, 25

Napoli Sotterranea 12, 44
nightlife 144-5
Notte delle Lampare 25

O
off-beat Naples 30-1
opening hours 145, 151
Oplontis 93
Ospedale delle Bambole 17, 30, 43

P
Palazzo dello Spagnuolo 69
Palazzo Mannajuolo 81
Palazzo Reale 55
Palazzo Reale di Capodimonte 17, 67
Palazzo Sanfelice 69
Parco Nazionale del Vesuvio 96
Parco Sommersa di Baia 148
Parco Vergiliano in Piedigrotta 89
Path of the Gods, the 14, 122-3
pharmacies 147
Piazza Bellini 43
Piazza Dante 58-9
Piazza dei Martiri 81
Piazza del Gesù Nuovo 43
Piazza del Plebiscito 59-60
Piazza Maradona 17, 54, 57
Piazza Mercato 49
Piazza Olmo 117
Piazza Sanità 69
Piazza Tasso 129
Piazza Umberto I 112-13
Piazzetta del Leone 89
Pio Monte della Misericordia 44
pizza Margherita 67
planning 22-3
Pompeii 12, 17, 90-5, **92**
population 151
Positano 16, 130-1, 136, 138, 139, **120-1**, **130**
prices 23, 29, 145
Procida 116-17, **116**
public holidays 151
public transport 27, 28-9
Punta Campanella Marine Reserve 14, 133
Punta di Tragara 17, 111

Q
Quartieri Spagnoli, see Toledo & Quartieri Spagnoli

R
Ravello 124-7, **126**
Ravello Festival 11, 24, 126-7
Real Albergo dei Poveri 45
Reggia di Caserta 102-3
Regio IX 95
responsible travel 60, 148-9
restaurants, see food, Eating subindex
Ricordo Di Mattia Fagnoni Mural 57
rideshares 28
Rifugio Santa Maria dei Monti 134
Ripley 136
Royal Chapel 55
Royal Park 102-3
Royal Wood 67
ruins, see archaeological sites & ruins

S
Sacello di Venere 101
safe travel 22, 147
Salto di Tiberio 108
San Domenico Maggiore 43
Santa Lucia & Chiaia 77-87, **78-9**
drinking 87
experiences 84-5
food 86-7
itineraries 80-1, 82-3, **80**, **82**
shopping 87
transport 77
walking tours 80-1, 82-3, **80**, **82**
Santa Maria dei Monti 14
Santa Maria delle Anime 43
scams 147
Seggiovia del Monte Solaro 113
Sentiero degli Dei 14, 122-3
shopping 10, 30, 149, see also individual neighbourhoods, Shopping subindex
soccer 11, 30, 54, 84
Sorrento (town) 128-9, 132, 137, 139, **120-1**, **128**
Sorrento Peninsula, see Amalfi Coast & Sorrento Peninsula
Spiaggia di Chiaia 16, 117
SSC Napoli 54
Stabiae 93
Stadio Diego Armando Maradona 11, 30, 84
Stazione dell'Arte 59
street art 17, 30, 44, 45, 57
sustainability 148-9
Swallow's Nest, the 127
swimming 16, 132

T
taxis 26, 28, 147
Teatro di Herculaneum 101
Teatro San Carlo 11, 60
Terme Centrali 100
Terra Murata 117
time zones 151
tipping 23, 144
Toledo & Quartieri Spagnoli 51-63, **52-3**
drinking 62-3
experiences 54-5, 58-60
food 61-2
highlights 54-5
itineraries 56-7, **56**
shopping 63
top experiences 54-5
transport 51
walking tours 56-7, **56**
Toledo Metro Station 17, 58
Totò 71
tours, see walking tours
train travel 26, 27, 28
transport 26, 27-9
travel seasons 24-5

U
Unauthorized Naples 44

V
vacations 151
Vallone dei Mulino 129
Veiled Christ 40-1
Via Emanuele de Deo 57
Via Krupp 112
Via Mezzacannone 30
Via San Gregorio Armeno 10, 30, 43
Vico Lungo del Gelso 57
Vico Totò 57
Villa Cimbrone 124
Villa Comunale 81
Villa dei Misteri 93-4

Villa Jovis 12, 108
Villa Maria 81
Villa Rufolo 124
Villa San Michele 108-9

walking, *see* hiking, walking tours
walking tours
   Capri Town & the Isle of Capri 110-11, **110**
   Centro Storico 42-3, **42**
   La Sanità 68-9, **68**
   Mercato & Borgo Orefici 48-9, **48**
   Mergellina 88-9, **88**
   Positano 130-1, **130**
   Procida 116-17, **116**
   Quartieri Spagnoli 56-7, **56**
   Ravello 127
   Santa Lucia & Chiaia 80-1, 82-3, **80, 82**
   Sorrento 128-9, **128**
water 147
weather 24
websites 146, 148, 150
wifi 151
wine 8-9, 97
women travellers 147

 Eating

86 Bistro 137

Acqu' e Sale 137
Acquapazza Cetara 138
Al Convento 138
Antica Pizza Fritta da Zia Esterina Sorbillo 62
Antica Pizzeria Di Matteo 46
Antica Pizzeria e Trattoria al '22 62
Antichissima Pizzeria Port'Alba 1738 46
Aria 46
Aumm Aumm 114

Babel 126

Caffe' Manari 114
Calamore 114
Cantina del Gallo 72
Capri Cakes 114
Carlo Fiamma 138
Casa d' 'e Femminielli 61
Casa Mele 138
Caseficio Starace 133
Caseificio Fernando De Gennaro 132-3
C'era Una Volta 138
Chalet Ciro 89
Chiosco sul Sentiero degli Dei 123
Cibi Cotti 86, 89
Cioccolato Mario Gallucci 73
Club Nautico della Vela 84-5, 86
Con Mollica o Senza 62
Concettina ai Tre Santi 72
CrudoRe 86
Cuore di Pane 129

Da Salvatore 126
Dialetti 86
Don Alfonso 1890 137
Donna Rosa 131

Eughenes 137

Gelateria Buonacore 113
Gennaro Amitrano 114
Gino Sorbillo Antica Pizzeria 46
Guarracino 137

Hosteria Toledo 61

I Masanielli di Francesco Martucci 103
Il Gelato Mennella 62
Isabella de Cham Pizza Fritta 72

Januarius 46

La Cambusa 138
La Cantinaccia del Popolo 137
La Capannina 114

La Locanda del Monacone 72
La Locanda Gesù Vecchio 46
La Passione di Sofi 61
La Salumeria 137
La Taverna di Totò 72
La Terrazza di Lucullo 115
Le Zendraglie 61
L'Ebbrezza di Noè 86
Lo Scoglio 137
Lo Sfizio 109
Lo Zaffiro 114
Lombardi 1892 72

Next2 138

O' cuop sapurit friggitoria 62
'O Cuzzetiello 46
'O Sfizio 61
'O Tabaccaro 86-7
O' Vascio 61
Officina del Mare 86
O'Parrucchiano La Favorita 137

Pasticceria Di Costanzo 73
Pasticceria Mignone 73
Pasticceria Poppella 73
Pescheria Le Botteghe 114
Pescheria Mattiucci 87
Pintauro 62
Pizzeria da Attilio 62
Pizzeria Donna Stella 138
Pizzeria Miracoli F.lli Esposito 72
Pizzeria Oliva di Carla e Salvatore 72
Pizzeria Starita 72
Pizzeria Trattoria La Taverna del Re a Capodimonte 72

Ristorante 34 da Lucia 138
Ristorante Da Adolfo 136
Ristorante il Saraceno d'Oro 138
Ristorante La Caravella 138
Ristorante La Zagara 115
Ristorante Mattozzi 61
Ristorante Vineria Cap'alice 86

Salumeria Aldo 114
Salumeria Malinconico 61

Sasà Martucci I Masanielli 103
Sesta Stazione 138
Sfogliate e Sfogliatelle 46
Sfogliatella Mary 62
Sfogliatelle Attanasio 46
Signora Bettola 86
Snack Bar da Antonio 114
Sorbillo Pizza a Portafoglio 62
Spuzzuliann pe' Tuledo 61

Tandem 46
Torre del Saracino 137
Trattoria A Pignata 61
Trattoria Addù Rosettin 72-3
Trattoria da Nennella 61
Trattoria dei Cartari 137
Trattoria dell'Oca 86
Trattoria Il Solitario 114

Viva Lo Re 100

Zi'Caterina 91

 Drinking

Anthill Cocktail Bar & Tapas 63
Antica Cantina Sepe 73
A'picio Spritz 63
Astronomia Bar Segreto 63

Bar dal Cavaliere 117
Bar degli Artisti 115
Bar della Valle 119
Bar Internazionale 131, 139
Bar Mexico 46
Bar Nilo 47
Bar Plaza 115
Barril 87
Bianca by La Palma 115

Caffè Ciorfito 47
Caffè del Principe 73
Caffè Gambrinus 62
Caffetteria Santoro 73

Cammarota Spritz 63
Cantina Central 92 47
Cantine Marisa Cuomo 135-6
Cantine Sociali 87
Chandelier 87
Cuccuma Caffè 47

Don Café Street Art Coffee 62

El Pocho Pub 73
Enoteca Belledonne 87
Ex Falegnameria 62

Fly 139
Franco's Bar 139

Giardino Mediterraneo 115
Gran Caffè 138

Hangout Capri 115

Il Riccio Sea Lounge 115
Il Vero Bar del Professore 62

La Bodega de D1OS 63
L'Antiquario 83, 87
Libreria Berisio 47

Malocchio 63
Masianello Art Cafe 139

Pansa 138

Sorrentino Vini 8, 97
Spazio Nea 47
Spuzzulè Winebar 63

Taverna Anema e Core 115
Terrace Bar, The 139
Terrace Bar at Hotel Caesar
  Augustus, The 115

 Shopping

Ars Neapolitana 47
Barbarulo Napoli 83
Biagio Barile 139
Bottega 21 47
Camiceria Piccolo 83
Carthusia 10
Carthusia I Profumi di Capri 112
Ceramica Artistica Solimene
  134-5
Ceramica Pinto 10, 134
Ceramiche Maria Grazia 139
Chiaja Vintage 87
Cilento 83
DieciDieci 63
E Marinella 10, 83, 84
Farella Capri 115
Ferrigno 47
Fratelli D'Angelo di Donato 49
Galleria Umberto I 59
Gay Odin 63
Gino Ramaglia 63
Happy Vintage 87
Jamón 47
JP Boutique 139
La Bottega di Brunella 139
La Botteguccia de Giovanni 139
La Capannina Più 115
La Fabbrica delle Meraviglie 63
La Scarabattola 47
La Scuderia del Duca 139
L'Altra Costiera 139
Magici Sentier 122
Mariano Rubinacci 83
Mastellone 10, 139
Materia Mediterranea 47
Mercato dei Vergini 73
Mercato di Resina 101
Mondadori 63
Omega 73
Pama Vintage 87
Piazzetta Orefici 49
Scriptura 47
Stinga Tarsia 139
Talarico 63
Vincenzo Oste Gioielli 73
Yam Capri 115

Ventimetriquadri 75

Send Us Your Feedback

We love to hear from travellers – your comments help make our books better. We read every word, and we guarantee that your feedback goes straight to the authors. Visit lonelyplanet.com/contact to submit your updates and suggestions.

Note: We may edit, reproduce and incorporate your comments in Lonely Planet products such as guidebooks, websites and digital products, so let us know if you are happy to have your name acknowledged. For a copy of our privacy policy visit lonelyplanet.com/legal.

Acknowledgements

Cover photograph: Amalfi, the Amalfi Coast (p119). Aleh Varanishchaa/Getty Images ©

Back cover photograph: Pompeii (p90). A-Babe/Shutterstock©

THIS BOOK

Destination Editor
Daniel Bolger

Cartographer
Rachel Imeson

Production Editor
Katie Connolly

Book Designer
Dominic Allen

Assisting Editor
Natalie Butler

Cover Researcher
Lauren Egan

Thanks to Shauna Daly, Jenna Myers, Charlotte Orr

Although the authors and Lonely Planet have taken all reasonable care in preparing this book, we make no warranty about the accuracy or completeness of its content and, to the maximum extent permitted, disclaim all liability arising from its use.

All rights reserved. No part of this publication may be copied, stored in a retrieval system, or transmitted in any form by any means, electronic, mechanical, recording or otherwise, except brief extracts for the purpose of review, and no part of this publication may be sold or hired, without the written permission of the publisher. Lonely Planet and the Lonely Planet logo are trademarks of Lonely Planet and are registered in the US Patent and Trademark Office and in other countries. Lonely Planet does not allow its name or logo to be appropriated by commercial establishments, such as retailers, restaurants or hotels. Please let us know of any misuses: lonelyplanet.com/legal/intellectual-property.

Paper in this book is certified against the Forest Stewardship Council™ standards. FSC™ promotes environmentally responsible, socially beneficial and economically viable management of the world's forests.

Published by Lonely Planet Global Limited
CRN 554153
3rd edition – Apr 2025
ISBN 978 1 83758 340 9
© Lonely Planet 2025
Photographs © as indicated 2025
10 9 8 7 6 5 4 3 2
Printed in China